NOT ALL HEROES
WEAR CAPES

JONO LANCASTER
NOT ALL
HEROES
WEAR CAPES

The incredible story of
how one young man
found happiness by
embracing his
differences

1

Ebury Press, an imprint of Ebury Publishing
20 Vauxhall Bridge Road
London SW1V 2SA

Ebury Press is part of the Penguin Random House group of companies
whose addresses can be found at global.penguinrandomhouse.com

First published by Ebury Press in 2023

www.penguin.co.uk

A CIP catalogue record for this book is available from the British Library

ISBN 9781529149357

Typeset in 11/18pt ITC Galliard Pro by Jouve (UK), Milton Keynes
Printed and bound in Great Britain by Clays Ltd, Elcograf S.p.A.

The authorised representative in the EEA is Penguin Random House Ireland,
Morrison Chambers, 32 Nassau Street, Dublin D02 YH68

Penguin Random House is committed to a
sustainable future for our business, our readers
and our planet. This book is made from Forest
Stewardship Council® certified paper.

Dedicated to all those that have felt that their true self doesn't fit in or belong in this world. I promise you — WE do!

CONTENTS

Introduction   1

Chapter 1 Wait, Am I Different?   11
Chapter 2 Why Me?   35
Chapter 3 In Trouble, Again?   51
Chapter 4 Someone Is Better than No One?   65
Chapter 5 Does Anybody Even Care?   87
Chapter 6 Fake It till You Make It?   101
Chapter 7 There's a Superhero Inside of You   139
Chapter 8 Look at How Far You've Come . . .   159
Chapter 9 Less Is More?   183
Chapter 10 What *Really* Is Self-Love?   189
Chapter 11 Healing Thoughts   195

Further Resources   203
Acknowledgements   207

INTRODUCTION

When I was 14 years old, my mum would give me £5 to go to the hairdresser's while she did the 'big shop' in town. Being the good lad that I was, I'd walk to the bus stop with my mum and make sure she got on the bus safely and then I'd wave goodbye.

Once the bus was out of sight, and with the £5 note in my hand, instead of going to the hairdresser's I'd head back home. I already knew what I was going to do as I had done it several times before.

Once I got home, the house empty except for me, I headed to the kitchen. I got the big scissors out of the top drawer under the kettle and went to the bathroom. I looked into the mirror and, with a big sigh, I began to cut my own hair.

Here are the ten steps I used to give myself the bowl cut that dominated the 1990s:

1. Tilt your head to the left, so that your hair hangs to one side. Cut the underneath parts on the left side.

2. Then tilt your head to the right, so that your hair hangs in the other direction. Cut the under parts of the right side. (You have now created the core elements of the 'undercut'.)

3. Run a wet comb through your hair, styling it 'on point'. A photo of Nick Carter from the Backstreet Boys will provide inspiration.

4. Curtains or bowl? Now's the time to make that decision.

5. If, like me, you choose bowl, slowly cut around your entire head in a 'straight' line. Try to use the comb as your guide to achieve this.

6. Grab a small mirror and look at the back of your head. Cut your neck hair as close to the skin as you can. Repeat this step a *lot*.

7. Smile at your badass self and admire your epic work. Now clean the bathroom from top to bottom, removing any trace of hair. Bleach the loo, scrub the tub and polish the mirror while you are in there. (This is important, see step 10.)

8. Don't look in the mirror for another six to eight weeks.

9. Go and buy £5 worth of football stickers (or any other treats you might be craving), then go and meet Mum off the bus, to help carry the shopping home.

10. Explain to Mum why you keep on going to the same shit hairdresser's and, to change the topic of the conversation, tell her that you've cleaned the bathroom from top to bottom just for her.

You'd be forgiven for thinking, *This is a book on self-love, not dodgy haircuts*, but the reason I did the above routine was not for the football stickers, not for the treats and, believe it or not, not even to clean the bathroom.

The reason why I cut my own hair was because I had a fear of the hairdresser's. I hated sitting on that chair in front of what felt like the world's biggest mirror, staring at my very own face, which I hated more than anything in this world.

Those were the feelings that dominated my teenage years as I often thought, *Why do I have to look like this?*

I was born with a condition called Treacher Collins syndrome, which affects 1 in 10,000–50,000 people (though some cases go undiagnosed). There are situations where the condition is inherited, but I was a 'sporadic mutation', meaning there was no family history of Treacher Collins. So, when I was born, it was a complete surprise to everyone that I looked a little different.

Treacher Collins only affects the facial features and presents itself differently in every person. In my case, I have no cheekbones, which means my eyes droop downwards. My ears haven't developed fully and so I have these cool little Bart Simpson-like ears, which means I am hard of hearing and wear a hearing aid to help me. My jaw and airway are also small, which for me just means that I snore when I sleep; but for others where this symptom is more severe, it can mean that they need support to breathe and eat, and surgery may be required to support daily life or even to maintain life.

By the time I had reached my teenage years and I was trusted to go to the hairdresser's by myself, I had come to look at my face and think, *Why the hell did this have to happen to me?*

Thankfully, a lot has changed in my life since those days of dodging the hairdresser's. My face hasn't changed, but my world has. I've gone from being consumed by feelings of shame to now being full of self-love, living in a world that's pretty colourful, surrounded by the best people and having some epic adventures.

Along the way, I've done a lot of work myself, but there have also been some incredible people in my life, from strangers to friends and family. I've come to realise, through experience, that not all heroes wear capes, and the kindness, generosity and love shown to me by these people have combined to make me who I am today.

There is also, however, one capeless hero in your life

who you might never have truly appreciated before: *you*. It's taken me years (and I'm still working on it!) to better understand that I can be my own hero, but it has been life-changing. Taking the time and putting in the effort to love myself more has transformed how I experience the world and I am certainly a happier person because of it.

This is why I want to share my story with you. While you might not have a facial difference like me, you might still feel like you don't quite 'fit in'. Maybe because you behave in a way some people don't understand, or you like doing things that are seen as 'uncool' or 'weird'. Whatever it is and whoever you are, I want you to see how self-love can shape your life for the better. And I want to let you in on the ways I've developed more confidence and more self-worth over the years, in case these tactics work for you too.

I've been lucky enough to help families and individuals all over the world to cope with challenges that sometimes made it feel difficult for them to love themselves, and I have set up a charity, which I'll tell you about later on. It's been amazing to see others grow, and through this book I want to help you find ways to gain confidence and to love and value yourself.

I never want you to feel as alone as I did, and while some days I still feel sad, angry or hurt, I know that, deep down, I love myself – and you should too.

5

A NOTE ABOUT MY FIRST HERO

There are times, especially when we are younger, when we need guidance more than ever, and we need a 'hero' to kick-start it all. From there we evolve, and we truly can become our own hero.

So, before I became my own hero, I needed another person to prompt it all for me: this turned out to be a lady called Jean.

At 40 years old, when I first met her, Jean was a short woman with short, wavy black hair and brown eyes. She had raised a family of two kids and moved on from her husband. She lived in a council house in Yorkshire. Her own children had grown up and moved out and so she began to invest her love in those that needed it most. In those who didn't have a home. And some (including myself) who didn't have a family.

Jean was a foster mum and she welcomed so many children into her home and into her heart. Whatever their background, she hugged, she cared, she loved. And to this day, despite being in her eighties, she continues to do so. She is the epitome of selflessness, kindness, love and heroism. The world is full of incredible, inspiring women and I feel truly blessed to have been introduced to one at such a young age.

Because of her, I'm the man I am today.

Jean was introduced to me when I was two weeks old, while social services were working on finding someone to care for me because my birth parents felt it was best to go our separate ways. At first nobody knew how I was going to develop mentally or physically. Many health professionals were involved, but there were very few clear words or thoughts on what the future might have in store for me.

Social services presented Jean with all this information and asked her if she would like to visit me in the hospital. Jean absolutely loved babies, so it was a no-brainer. 'Yes, of course I would.'

'He looks different. Please be prepared for the way he looks,' warned social services.

Jean came to visit me anyway.

Jean stands tall but she doesn't even reach five foot, so most things fly over her head, especially words like that.

So, Jean met me when I was only 14 days old in the hospital, and she saw me and couldn't help but smile. She asked the nurses if she could hold me. They said yes and handed me to her. In that moment, she felt a connection, a bond, and she turned to the nurses and asked, 'When can I take him home?'

Jean would foster me for the next five years, and she, her grown biological children (Claire and Stephen) and the rest of their family cared for me in every way I needed:

hospital appointments, nursery visits, play dates, smelly nappies – the lot. They gave me the best foundation to grow, but more importantly, they gave me a second chance at being a part of a family.

We lived in a three-bedroom council house in West Yorkshire, in a little village called Featherstone, famous for its rugby league and flat caps. It was the sort of place where everyone knew each other, and everyone surely knew us. The house with all the kids in it, looked after by a hero without a cape.

At home, Mum always slept downstairs on the sofa. I had my bedroom with bunk beds in it that was often shared with another boy that Mum fostered. The other bedroom was for girls, so they had their privacy, and Mum had her own room but for some reason never used it. (It became more of a storage place for all the things we owned; Mum didn't throw anything away. In this bedroom you would find old school reports, newspaper clippings of our sports games, school photos, spare cots, old toys for all ages, clothes, trophies from our weekend sport clubs. It was a treasure-trove of memories.)

Our street was full of young families, so you'd often see all the kids playing outside. The houses were in lines of four, with ginnels to either side that you could cut through. We had three small greens around the back that we named Wembley, Old Trafford and Elland Road because they

8

were our very own football fields! We also had allotments at the end of the street, surrounded by trees that we built our dens in.

It was home – our home, our safe place.

I was placed for adoption when I was four years old, but due to Jean's lack of income, not owning her own home and being divorced, social services were reluctant to legally fully sign me over to Jean and her family. However, after a lot of fighting and love from Jean and her family, I was officially adopted by them on 18 May 1990. I was lucky to have found my forever family and I became a Lancaster. We celebrated with a party and even to this day we continue to celebrate that date.

Jean was the person who gave me a fresh start in the world. While this book will celebrate you and guide you to recognise how truly special you are, as a child we often need love to be introduced to us.

Throughout the book, you'll find some prompts and exercises that I've used over the years to help me build my own sense of self-love. I'm including them in the pages of my story in case you'd like to try them too.

To kick us off, take a moment to think about who showed you love and kindness when you were a child. Have you ever thanked them? Have you shown them your appreciation? Let's do that now: write down some of the early heroes in your life and send some love and gratitude their way. As an adult we can forget all those that supported us when we were younger!

If you are still in contact with them, how about sending them a little note of gratitude?

CHAPTER 1
WAIT, AM I DIFFERENT?

Looking back, as a child I didn't know that I looked different. In some ways, this was amazing. I could enjoy being a child, feeling carefree, and like I 'fitted in' with the rest of my class. But it also meant that I didn't do any work to build my confidence, because I didn't know any work needed to be done.

It can be really tempting to try and recreate that childhood feeling of not knowing about your problems as an adult. You may want to go back to those days of not realising that you've got stuff to deal with, not even realising that you're different in some way. We can turn a blind eye to our problems as an avoidance strategy. But if we never deal with our pains, later on in our lives they can come out and erupt, potentially causing even more damage and trauma than if we'd dealt with them promptly. This can be crushing when our lives feel settled. It's like: *Where did that come from? Oh, the shit that I ignored years ago . . .*

I wasn't doing this on purpose when I was younger, but I definitely didn't see what was in store for me over the following years.

When I think back, I always knew I was adopted. There was never a moment when I was sat down and told; as far as I can remember, I had always known and throughout my early years it was explained to me with words that I would understand. Mum would share that she met me at the hospital, that she spoke to Claire and Stephen (now my brother and sister) and they had all decided that I could come live with them. She went on to explain that some parents become parents in lots of different ways and this was our way. I loved that story: that was *our* story!

On the anniversary of my adoption day each year, we would celebrate with a party. Mum would invite all my friends over, I would have a cake and a few presents – it was a true celebration. It felt like I had two birthdays throughout the year, with two sets of presents. (That's pretty frigging cool for a kid!) It was my normal.

And so I never felt out of place being adopted; and even when it came to my face, I didn't feel different. I didn't see or think that I was different.

This is hugely down to my mum. She treated me like everyone else and celebrated me in my own way. She celebrated others in their own unique ways too. She fostered children with all kinds of different needs. Some had autism, while others had wheelchairs. We were all different and yet all the same, and through that, I naturally grew up celebrating who I was.

It's clear to me now that Mum wanted me to enjoy the innocence of being a child while I still could. Maybe she knew what negativity lay ahead and wanted me to be prepared for it, but I think she also wanted me not to fear for my future too. I can't even begin to imagine the pressure on her, and the emotional struggle going on inside her must have been tough; but every question and any wandering thought that I had about my background or how I looked, my mum never avoided it. She recognised how I felt, thought about it and answered. She has such a huge heart, she can feel everything you say.

In nursery and then primary school, everyone knew who I was and I had plenty of friends. I was Jono, one of the kids in the class.

As a kid, I loved playing out in the street, making potions with the water I took from a grate right outside my house. We built epic dens from the items we found in the streets beside the allotments. We made toy guns out of sticks and played soldiers, running through the ginnels shouting '*pew pew!*' as we shot each other.

And those games of football on 'our' pitches – they were epic, last goal wins!

When we weren't playing outside, I would be found in my bedroom playing on my computer. I would take off my hearing aids when Mum was shouting at me to tidy my room or when I wanted an extra 15 minutes on the Nintendo. 'Sorry, Mum, I didn't hear you!'

This was normality for me. I even developed a habit of removing my hearing aids whenever I felt scared, as if not being able to hear the scary stuff meant it wasn't there. (I guess this is kinda true in life, don't you think?)

During this time, I'm sure so many negative things happened around me. I just didn't see them as I wasn't aware. I didn't look for them, I didn't feel them, I didn't know they even existed.

I've learned as an adult, through my charity, that I was exceptionally lucky to be this way. I spend a lot of time now with new parents who have children with various medical needs and the conversations that I have with them are often crushing.

A common thing they share is that from birth many health professionals, intentionally or not, prevent parents from forming a nurturing bond with a medically dependent child in those first few moments. The child gets whisked away. 'Don't worry,' they say. 'Don't look.' And then there's a whisper to their colleagues, 'Did anything appear on the scans?' This leaves parents confused and, most of all, frightened. 'What's wrong with my child? Why can't I see them?'

Those first few moments of our life are an important bonding point, and are often neglected and at times not granted to parents with a medically dependent child.

I can't help but wonder now what happened at my birth. *How was I presented to my birth parents? What were they told? What bonding were they able to do in those hours they were with me?*

For the first few years of our lives, our guardians, our parents, the ones who raise us, see and feel it all and somehow magically shield us from all the pain. My mum did an excellent job at that, but I know it's not easy. Again, from conversations with new parents, I can hear and understand that they're anxious about their child playing out in the street, getting bullied at school, not getting invited to birthday parties, or having other parents or adults asking, 'What's wrong with your baby?'

This all makes me appreciate the fact that I grew up without even feeling this. Perhaps a small part of me wishes that my mum had spoken to me about some of the things she felt. As humans we find it normal to talk about positive things, but unfortunately it's not normal to talk about the things that upset us, make us feel sad or make us angry.

These conversations need to be normalised from a

much younger age, and if that had happened for me, then maybe I wouldn't have felt so guilty when I did finally open up. Maybe I wouldn't have pushed away those who tried to help me, because it would have been normal to talk about these things and ask for help.

But our guardians aren't prepared for any of this and so they do an incredible job at guiding us and protecting us with every bit of love they have. Love and strength that I'm sure they didn't even know they had.

From this point on, I want you to try to normalise all the feelings that you have and, if you're in a safe space, share them with those around you. Stop apologising for 'bringing the mood down'. Yes, there are better times when we can talk about certain topics, but please start sharing the 'negatives' just like you would when you happily talk about having a great day.

I want you to think about this past week and write down some of the things that you could/should have said to those around you, but you didn't because the mood or the timing wasn't right.

Now ask yourself: would they have listened to you?

They probably would have! They would have listened, and if you wanted to receive some advice or information they might have been able to support you.

So, let's get into the habit of speaking. Sometimes just saying something out loud is enough to help us process, and sometimes we'll share in the hope we can get some guidance and support back!

Try to remember this the next time you're experiencing negative feelings.

Outside of day-to-day life and school, I had so many health appointments that I needed to attend that were linked to Treacher Collins. These included the ENT (ear, nose and throat) appointments where a health professional looked at the structure and formation of my skull to assess the quality of my hearing and breathing; speech therapy, as my lack of hearing meant my speech was delayed; and regular tests to assess what I could and couldn't hear. Again, this was my normal – I thought everyone had some appointments going on. All the other kids we cared for sure did.

The hospital appointments were annoying, though. I had to have the day off school, usually on the days we did PE (I loved PE), and the trip to London involved a 5am start to catch the 6am train down south. Mum even asked the school to give me schoolwork to do on the journey, which always seemed to be maths (I hated maths). The only comfort I had on the trains was that at some point on the way there I was allowed a microwavable pepperoni pizza from the train kitchen (I really loved pizza).

After two hours, the maths had been completed, the pizza enjoyed, and we had arrived in London.

We always headed straight to the hospital. Once we got there, while Mum went to the reception desk, I'd hope for five minutes with the electronic bus-driving game at the main entrance. I'd get so jealous if someone else was on it. *Come on, it's my turn now!*

Speech therapy would often come first. A health professional from London would sit to face me and with their weird southern accent they would say words that I had to repeat. Due to their accent and my lack of hearing it was a lot of guesswork from myself, but then they'd be like 'That's great, Jono. Now we're going to do this with my back to you.' *Oh no*, I'd think. *I've been rumbled.* Lip-reading was my secret talent and now I couldn't do that! The speech therapy would then continue with the Londoner's back to me, even more guesswork, and by then I was certain I was saying words that don't belong in the English language!

But once we had finished, nothing but praise was sent my way and I left with a proud smile – *Aced it!* I thought.

Next up would be the hearing tests. After explaining to me what would happen they asked me to remove my hearing aid and in exchange they gave me these giant headphones to wear that felt so heavy on my little head. These where wired to a machine and all I had to do now was listen – while trying to keep this massive hearing device on my head!

They pressed a button that would send a sound to the headpiece at different frequencies and when I heard that sound I had to place a wooden block from one basket into another. As a child, this was fun; as a teenager, it was the lamest thing I ever had to do.

The maddest thing was that the volume would start at a high frequency, which was so loud and obvious that I would confidently move a wooden block. *I'm acing this!* I thought. The volume would then get lower and lower. During the lower sounds my head would play all kinds of tricks on me and to this day it still does. When there is silence, sometimes my head fills it with noise. There have been times when I've been in bed with my hearing aid off, falling asleep, then all of a sudden I hear an alarm going off. I wake up and put my hearing aid on, but there's no alarm, just silence.

So, during these hearing tests, when the low volumes were played I'd be asking myself, *Is that a sound or is that in my head?* I would hear a buzz and press down on the button and wait for the next sound before thinking I'd hear a new buzz. *I won't press just yet though in case it's not real.* But then I hadn't pressed my button for the longest ten seconds ever and the hearing person was just staring at me. *Surely I need to press it now?* Instead of doing a hearing test, I ended up participating in a guessing game, with the prize being a hearing aid that was properly tuned in to my personal 'accurate' hearing scores!

If I wasn't having tests done, I was having surgeries. My mum always involved me in these decisions and discussions, but the general rule was that if it was going to improve my health we'd do it. When it came to the cosmetic surgeries, I was always asked how I felt about them. I was a child, so I didn't really understand the magnitude of talking about surgery to improve my face, so I would say 'No, my face is ace.' To my mind, nothing bad had ever happened because of my face – I was blissfully unaware. I especially loved the shape of my ears!

Although I thought my ears were cool, I had to wear my hearing aids on a hairband as a child. As a boy with a shaved head, unsurprisingly, I hated it. They rubbed against my skin and always felt so uncomfortable. And, oh God, when it rained! I remember my mum would have these plastic hair bonnets that old ladies used to use, and she would make me wear one. *Come on, Mum.* I needed some cool points and this didn't help.

As I got older and my skull became stronger and thicker, it was decided that I would have a bone-anchored hearing aid, which basically involved a screw being drilled into the side of my head near my ear with the end poking out. Once that had healed, my hearing aid was attached to the screw like a press stud, and there we go: no headband and no more plastic bags on my head when it rained. Now a regular hood would work to keep a more discreet hearing aid dry. Happy days.

However, to perform this hearing aid surgery, it was back to London. More maths and more pizza. I kind of loved hospital days. I was able to play on a Nintendo and I was waited on hand and foot. I even had my first crush at the hospital: a nurse called Rachel would buy football stickers for me and during her shift we would swap and stick them in our sticker books. I thought she was the coolest person, and that simple act of kindness has stayed with me ever since.

Before my surgeries, I remember not being able to eat or drink anything. A numbing cream was rubbed on my hands and cannulas inserted, and then I was given a green liquid that would send me to sleep. I was always able to choose a toy to take with me as I was wheeled down to the surgery room and, with a limited choice from the hospital collection, I always chose Skeletor from *He-Man*.

I remember lying down on the hospital bed, watching the ceiling roll by, hearing random voices, seeing the odd adult look down and smile, all while holding on to Skeletor. I wasn't scared, I wasn't nervous, this was just my life.

The next thing I knew, I'd wake up with an intense desire to pee.

'I need the toilet,' I'd say urgently. Nothing else mattered to me in that moment – I just needed to pee. So I started trying to get up, but was quickly told, 'Lie down, Jonathan, you're too unstable. We'll get you a bottle.' The bottle was passed to me and I was very unhappy about the idea of using it. After quite a bit of moaning, I finally worked up the courage to go in the bottle (or maybe my need to pee became too strong!) and I could, at last, relax.

After this ordeal, I composed myself, felt the bandages around my head, my dry mouth and my belly rumbling. Skeletor was nowhere to be seen and I realised I was hungry. The staff would bring me chocolate milk and spaghetti hoops, as they always did, and then I knew that I was OK.

The surgeon eventually came round and told us the surgery had gone well and that tomorrow I would be able to return home. Once healed, I would need to come back, and after a check-up I'd be able to wear my new hearing aid.

So I rested, and swapped more stickers with Rachel the nurse. The final thing after surgery visits was the removal of the cannula. Pulling the plasters off, they would leave these dollops of cream on my hand and the one thing I hated about the whole thing was this cream – I couldn't even look at it. Still to this day, I get uncomfortable around other people using skin creams.

Eventually, then, I got my new hearing aids and I thought they were the coolest thing. I coud hear so much better and so much more clearly, but ultimately I also looked so much cooler without the headband.

After every appointment in London, whether it was for testing, surgery or a routine check-up, we gathered our things and went over to the finance window. It was a single window along a plain white corridor and I sat on a chair, watching my mum gather every receipt she had from the day to try and reclaim some travel expenses.

We lived in a council house and, as my mum didn't have a job, money was tight, despite us living up north where things were less expensive. So a trip to London, where prices are even higher, crippled us. Every penny counted in the Lancaster household. I was oblivious to this as a child. I just couldn't wait for what adventure Mum had in store for us next.

Mum would signal to me that it was time to go and I'd grab my coat. She collected whatever money she could recoup, and we'd leave the hospital.

Because Mum would always try to save every penny she had, after our appointments at Great Ormond Street Hospital we would go somewhere cool: Covent Garden, Piccadilly Circus, Harrods, the museums, pizza places – Mum didn't hold back; we did it all, via the Tube.

I have so many happy memories of street performers at

Covent Garden, seeing all the advertisements at Piccadilly Circus, trying to find the cheapest toy at Harrods, visiting museums with a room full of stars and sampling London's finest pizzas.

Around 7pm we would head back to King's Cross station and we would get the 8pm train back up north. More maths and – you've guessed it – one final pizza! We'd get home around 10pm, both shattered, but ultimately I was happy and crazily excited to tell everyone about our trip. It was worth missing PE for!

Back at school, I'd tell all my teachers and mates that I had been to London. I'd share my new adventures and even tell them about my new hearing aids that were magically tuned into my hearing based on those 'accurate' results.

When the kids at school asked about my latest hearing aids, I was happy to talk about them and show them the new design. They were most impressed by the gold screw drilled into my head.

I'd even pretend that I could use them as a calculator and that if they got wet they would blow up the entire school. It's easier in the younger years at school to impress your mates. Imagination helps us all get along, don't you think?

Looking back, I naturally celebrated my life with so much love and joy.

Love and joy should be a natural part of life, especially when you're a child.

Would you have eaten pizza for every meal if you could? Were you also obsessed with PE and sticker books? Or would you have invented a story about blowing up your school?

Think about your own childhood and what you loved about yourself as a child. What were your quirks? What stories and games did you play? What can you remember being like as a child that makes you smile now?

Now here is a question for you: those things that you once loved, why don't you do them any more? What's stopping you from sharing and celebrating those quirks you once were proud of?

As we get older our lives can become so stressful and serious. If we could just take a moment now and then to be a kid again, I think that would be the best break from all the adulting that we do!

If you ever see me about, you'll see that I'm still a big kid at heart, celebrating all my quirks!

To others, it wasn't just my physical appearance that was different. My upbringing was also different. My home and family were different from those of my schoolfriends. I didn't know anyone else who was in and out of hospital. I didn't know anyone else who lived in a foster home whose inhabitants might change from year to year.

Even when kids asked why Mum was so old or why I didn't have a dad, my response was: 'Mum's not married, and when I was born I was left in a hospital. She visited and out of all the kids there, she chose me. Your mums and dads got stuck with you, but my mum chose me, which is just the coolest thing ever.'

I didn't think not having a dad was a bad thing, it was just something I didn't have. It was no big deal, I didn't know any different. But later in life, when I became aware of what a dad was or what I thought having a dad would add to my life, this caused me pain: another example of something hurting when I became more aware it existed.

But, ultimately, not knowing what life held ahead was a good thing. Mum always told me I was beautiful, and I believed it. She created a positive environment for me and everyone else that lived with us, and through that I naturally celebrated my life and who I was.

I also got asked who all the kids were that stayed with us, and what happened to them when they no longer lived with us.

I would happily answer that they were my foster brothers and sisters, and some had been reunited with their birth families, some had been adopted and some had gone to another foster home.

I can't express how lucky I feel to have had that family consistency in my life. I hate to think where I'd be without Jean.

I guess I became aware of my differences the older I got, but back then, at this time, I frigging loved them. I adored standing out and having my own quirks.

My mum continued to foster, and the house was always full of people, life and, at times, drama. We did every after-school club going and at the weekends Mum would always have chores for us all to do. But despite having four kids doing chores, the house always seemed to be a mess.

When we went anywhere it was like a military operation to get out of the house. Yes, we were always late, but we did have a routine to get us out of the door. Everyone had their slot for the bathroom or downstairs toilet, their own unique breakfast prep and their own uniform, depending on what school we attended, and out of the house we went, in organised chaos.

I remember the school holidays before I started high school. I was so excited about starting a new school. We had a new school uniform and we had to wear a blue blazer. I had never worn a blazer before, never mind owned one. We had to sew our school emblem patch over the front pocket of our blazer. This went with a white shirt, black trousers and a blue-and-white tie. We all got new school shoes, coats and bags, and carefully selected the coolest pencil case and stationery sets we could find.

Then the school holidays were over and high school began.

This was when things started to change.

As I got older, I started to notice that people would just stare at me. At school I began to see the older kids pointing, laughing, making comments, there were even the odd playground games of 'run away from him 'cos you'll get his disease'. This change in my peers felt like it had come out of nowhere and was totally unexpected. Just the day before I'd been impressing them with my explosive hearing aids and now I was a germ, a monster, the least cool person in the school. I started to see it everywhere, I even looked out for it, like I was on high alert.

One of the biggest '*oh, fuck*' moments involved the local school buses.

The area where I lived has the nickname 'the five towns', and these towns had school buses running throughout the whole area, collecting kids from their street and dropping them off at school in the morning, and vice versa when school was over.

They had always been there but I really saw and felt those buses when I started high school.

After a while we got into a morning routine and left the house at different times, meeting our individual friends along the way. As I walked to school, I always saw the buses doing their stops.

I can never forget one double-decker bus that had the kids with yellow school shirts in it. It seemed to know where I was and always chose the worst times to drive by me.

I would be waiting for the green man to appear on the signal so that I could cross the road when that big double-decker bus would stop at the lights, and the whole school bus stared at me. Kids would bang on windows and pull their eyes down, literally everyone would be laughing at me. It was like I was the special attraction and their windows were the viewing glass.

I hated that bus and I wanted to hide every time I saw it.

That was before school even started, so it was basically my first interaction of the day with the outside world. 'Good morning, Jonathan, and fuck you!'

As I got older, I remember Mum having conversations with me, explaining that when I was older and in a pub people might be unkind, but my response had always been 'No they won't.' Until junior school, it just didn't enter my mind that anybody would be unkind, despite her warnings. Now I felt my understanding of her words roll over me like an avalanche.

A few interactions in the playground were the first rumblings, but soon I noticed the stares and heard the comments more and more, everywhere I went, even at the places I loved to visit. They seemed worse – bigger and bigger boulders barrelling towards me – until I found myself completely buried under self-loathing. The once carefree and confident young lad felt the weight of society's judgement crushing the very heart in my chest, and this led me to ask: *why?*

The innocent unawareness had gone.

The things that I once celebrated with everyone around me soon became things that I was embarrassed and ashamed about.

This was when I really needed to start working on the self-love and on facing new challenges, unpicking the feelings that I was experiencing, talking about my emotions, learning to celebrate myself again, but where could I start? Who could guide me? I started to look everywhere and I would pray that safe, happy times lay ahead for me and my mum.

NOT ALL HEROES WEAR CAPES, BUT NOT ALL VILLAINS HAVE SCARS

As I began to look for guidance and hope I often looked at the media around me. From computer games to movies, I looked, I observed and I picked up quite a lot.

Hollywood has ingrained in our brains that villains more often than not look damaged on the outside. Bond villains often have a scar, the villain in *The Lion King*, for example, is named Scar. There are countless examples where having a facial difference is seen as a bad thing; something bad has happened that has caused pain and anger, and you are set to destroy the world because of those feelings. That's hugely false, hugely damaging, and for me, as a teenager, was hugely impactful.

When I looked for hope, I found defeat.

This trend also led me to falsely see good in 'good-looking' people when in fact, if you are going to call anyone a villain, a villain could look quite successful. They could be well appointed in life. They are villains because they know how to wield power over others for their own gain. It is so important to recognise this too, because in our search to fit in and find connection, we

31

NOT ALL HEROES WEAR CAPES

have to realise that the shiny, popular, charismatic crowd may not be the one to aspire to.

This is something I failed to see when I was a teenager.

As an adult I'm aware I still have a lot of healing to do, and at times I have found it easier to ignore certain feelings. I have avoided certain triggers – for example, I won't listen to certain songs that bring back unhappy memories or feelings. I'm very aware that there are periods of my life for which I don't have the capacity to do the healing or work that's required. So I try and create a sense of bliss, try not to think about it, try to occupy my mind, try not to explore it as I know it will hurt.

But the key for me now is that I always make sure I will visit a difficult thing when I feel prepared for it. Sometimes I need a push, but I will explore the feelings, I will sit with the pain and I will do the work, as ignoring it may seem easier at the time, but it usually explodes further down the line.

Are there any emotions, situations or even people that you're ignoring right now? What/who are they? Why are you ignoring them?

What's your next step in dealing with these situations or people?

Role-playing scenarios or going through them in your head can help. For example, I have role-played what I would do if a child were to see me and ask his mum or dad 'What's wrong with that man's face?' I have rehearsed this, experienced this and now feel that this scenario is more manageable, that I am more prepared for it if it happens. We can apply that to many scenarios in our life.

Lastly, what causes you stress and how do you manage that?

When we face a stressful situation, we often fail to complete the stress cycle, which needs to be done. For example, when a zebra is chased by a lion, it runs and, once safe, it will complete its stress cycle by shaking its whole body to release all that stress.

We can do the same: after a stressful situation you can play your favourite tunes and shake, dance, mosh, head bang, let it go.

Movement or exercise also works, as well as self-grooming, like brushing your hair, or getting a massage. All of these can help you complete your own stress cycle.

One stressful situation that I regularly face is speaking at events or in schools. It doesn't matter how many I do, they always cause stress, and once they're over I have this massive urge to sleep, which actually makes me feel even worse. Now I have got into the routine of moving afterwards – I will walk, I'll go to the gym or I will go through some yoga sequences.

Remember, after a stressful situation – shake it like a zebra!

CHAPTER 2
WHY ME?

After you've been through something traumatic or upsetting, have you ever just sat there and asked yourself, *Why me? Why did that happen? What have I done to deserve this?*

The 'why me?' question took over my life during my teenage years and consumed my entire thought process.

The 'why?' thoughts really started when I hit high school. My school, Featherstone High, was split into an upper school and a lower school, and when I first started we had a couple of weeks when it was just the first two year groups that would attend. I was around my friends, seeing kids that I had seen at football and rugby training. It was OK, but these two weeks quickly passed and then the three older years joined us.

From that point, I met so many other kids who had never seen me before and they were curious about me, to say the least. I still had my friends. I lost a few friends along the way too, which hurt, but I also made new friends too.

A note to myself – I have always been able to make friends, sometimes I have forgotten this!

During this period my mum still fostered other children, but now they went to specialist schools via taxis, so when I started high school that army of kids who had once set off for school with me had stopped and I was left to face those local school buses alone.

Mum took me to after-school clubs: football, rugby, swimming, snorkelling and – even with my big bobble head held up by my little sparrow body – weightlifting. At high school this helped as people in my year group knew of me already.

Mum still celebrated me, but I began to struggle to celebrate myself during high school.

After a tough day at school I would often go to my room, and I would close my bedroom door and stand in front of it so nobody could walk in. I put my hands together, closed my eyes and prayed. I don't know who I was reaching out to, I didn't know what I believed in, but I prayed for protection, I prayed for people to be kind to me, and I prayed that one day I would be OK.

This gave me hope.

But high school was tough and it was a daily grind against the older kids; they were horrible and I started to experience things that I'd never experienced or understood before.

The older kids continued to pull their eyes down to mimic mine. They would walk past and fold their ears down, again to mimic my own. They started teasing me about my birth parents, making fun of me because I was born on Halloween, inventing chants and songs about me and openly singing them in front of everyone.

It was extremely tough, and I wasn't mentally prepared for any of it.

I then started to see this at the after-school clubs and on the weekends. The stares and negativity seemed to creep into every aspect of my life.

My friend and I used to go to a snorkelling club after school. I was like a fish in water, I could swim and swim. I worked through all my life-saving badges and then progressed to deep-sea diving and snorkelling.

My favourite bit was getting a 25p pick 'n' mix afterwards. I always got a few extra ones as the mum running the stall had a soft spot for me.

In the snorkelling class, I was cruising through the badges and really enjoying it. I even enjoyed a trip up north and started doing open-water diving.

But things changed when an older boy started attending the class. He immediately started targeting me, pinching me under the water, putting his finger down my snorkel, pulling my mask off and grabbing my flippers. I hated him. In the changing rooms, he would openly talk about me in front of everyone and loudly ask:

'Why were you adopted again?'

'Why do you look like that?'

'What happened to your face?'

He would ask the same questions every week, changing the wording ever so slightly, and it hit a nerve because they were things I was asking myself and still trying to process.

I didn't tell anyone what was happening. My defence mechanism was to arrive early, avoid him, have a quick shower afterwards and leave early.

In my local swimming baths, the water was really cold, so the hot showers afterwards – especially in winter – were glorious.

One cold evening, after a tough snorkelling lesson, that hot shower felt extra special, and I completely lost track of time. I saw everyone else, including the older boy, getting out of the pool. I panicked and rushed to my locker, unlocked it, grabbed my clothes before I was properly dry and began to get dressed.

It was too late, though. The older boy was already in the changing rooms with me.

As I was putting on my trousers, I heard:

'*So-o-o-o*, tell us again just why it is you look like that?'

I ignored him.

He walked over and even his shadow overpowered me. He asked another question.

'Is your face the reason why you were adopted?'

That day I had heard that question once too often and I lost it. I pushed him away and ran. He didn't like that and he chased me. I ran into a cubicle and closed the door. They didn't have locks on them so I leaned against it with all my weight in the hope he couldn't get in.

He entered the next cubicle to me, stood on the bench and reached over to grab me.

I dropped low so he couldn't reach.

He gave up and just barged through the door and proceeded to slap me.

Once the teachers arrived, they soon pulled him away from me. Without saying anything, I put the rest of my clothes on, grabbed my towel and trunks and ran out to the area where the sweets were being sold. I cried like I had never cried before. And when my mum asked what had happened, I couldn't speak.

My friend stood by my side and told her everything.

The older boy was banned from coming to the class for

a few weeks, but the emotional damage had already been done and I didn't want to go any more either.

This event consumed me. The 'why?' thoughts consumed me. Why was this happening all of a sudden? Why did it feel like every day, everywhere I went, something bad seemed to happen?

Did all of that happen as I think it did, or was some of it in my imagination? Did I assume it was all negative? How had I missed all this when I was younger?

Once I was there, in that negative frame of mind, I found it very hard to get out of it, and that question hit me: *why me?* Why was this happening to me? What had I done to deserve this?

My little head tried to work it out, from the moment I woke to the very last thought I had before I eventually fell asleep. *Why me?*

I have a friend I've known all my life. We played football together and at home we loved watching *Teenage Mutant Ninja Turtles.* I was a big fan of the turtles and Raphael was my favourite. I even had the van that shot pizzas out from the front. (*More pizza.*)

We went through all the schools together and up into high school.

As we lived near each other, we would always walk home from high school together, talking football and turtles.

One day as we were walking home, debating how England could win the World Cup, the Year 11 lads were standing outside the chippy and we were walking towards them.

They saw us and started chanting: '*Toffee toffee toffee.*'

They were all pointing and laughing at us as we walked by.

Once we'd gone past and could no longer hear them, I asked my friend, 'What the hell was that about?' I didn't get it.

He looked down and struggled to get his words out as he didn't really know how to explain it.

'Mate, it's proper shit, but they sing that song about you, they think your hearing aid looks like a toffee sweet.'

Right at that moment I wanted the ground to swallow me up whole. It hurt that they were making fun of me, but it hurt even more that my friend knew too, had known for a long time, and until this moment I had been totally oblivious to it. I was crushed and embarrassed. What else was going on behind my back?

On the walk home, his house came up first and after he went inside, I walked the rest of the way home alone. I cried.

I was embarrassed, scared, confused as to why this was happening.

I got home and Mum was there, with the usual question: 'How's your day gone?'

'Yeah, all good,' was my instant reaction, and I headed to my room.

Alone in my room, I stood in front of the mirror and looked at my face, I thought about my birth parents, I said my prayer of hope and realised that I needed to talk to my mum about it.

As the evening went on, I waited and waited for the right time to ask her. I didn't want to make it obvious, so I tried to pick my moment and words carefully.

So I went to Mum, my hero, and asked her why people might be unkind to me. She asked if anything had happened, and I said no, I was just curious. But after recent events at the snorkelling class she was on high alert for these things, and she worked her way through areas of my life to try to catch me out.

'How's school?'

'How's football?'

'How are your friends?'

I got through the questions and hid almost all of my fears and thoughts.

For some reason I just couldn't share what I really wanted to share.

And as she always had done since the day she met

me, she built me up, and filled me with love and positivity.

The older kids continued to be mean at school. The double-decker-bus kids continued to laugh at me. I stopped going to the after-school clubs that I loved. I was struggling to process and accept the fact that my birth parents, the two people who are supposed to love you the most, had left me to deal with this all on my own. I continued to ask my mum the vague questions, and I think deep down she knew what was going on, but I would never say what had happened. I didn't know how to. I had no experience in talking about this stuff.

We had more conversations but the more we had, the more I stopped believing in Mum; I stopped believing in myself and I started to obsess about it and believe all the negativity around me and in my head.

In my bedroom I had a wardrobe with a mirror in the centre of it. I often found myself looking into that mirror and asking all kinds of questions.

Why me? Why do I look like this? Why did my birth parents leave me? Why are people being mean to me?

As I asked those questions, I stared at my face in the mirror, really focusing on my eyes. They were the things that I hated the most. With both hands, I pushed my eyes up and tried to imagine my face like everyone else's. *I'd be happy if I looked like this,* I thought. *Maybe if I do this for long enough, they'll stay a little straighter.*

I got so angry that I couldn't change my face. In my head I remembered surgeons talking to me about surgeries on my face. 'We can improve your face.' 'We can build you some cheekbones.'

As a teenager, my response was a straight 'no' with no explanation!

My internal thoughts, which I kept to myself, were: *I don't want my face 'improving', I want a new face.* I hated this one and no other surgery would help me.

I wanted to look like the actors I saw in films. I wanted to be the hero. I craved to be like the singers in all the boy bands that had all their adoring fans. I wish I had the confidence of the sports stars I saw in the stadiums. But most of all, I wanted to look like my friends.

And that was never going to happen. I was so far away from self-love, I stopped looking in the mirror. If I was out walking down the street and caught a glimpse of my face in a window, it was a harsh reality check that I looked different and I didn't belong, so I avoided the situation and tried to ignore it. I really needed a hero, but my safe places no longer felt safe as I had a head full of the worst thoughts that I took everywhere with me. I was a closed book, unable to share; I was beaten, and I was pushing people and my heroes away.

*

During this period, when I became obsessed with that 'why me?' question, no other information went in, nothing else mattered, I didn't care about anything else. That question held me back for so many years.

It wasn't just other school kids who made me feel othered, it was adults too.

One day, my mum and I were in London on the Tube, for one of my various medical appointments. It was my job to look at the maps and count down to our stop.

We were sitting there when I noticed a couple sat across from me. They were pretty into each other, holding hands, kissing – you know the couples that are OTT in public that make you think *Get a room* – but all I could think was: *One day I hope someone likes me in that way.*

So, I'm people-watching and feeling kind of important counting down the Tube stops so we wouldn't miss our stop.

Then I noticed the young couple staring at me and they began to laugh. They looked away and tried to hide their giggles, but every time they had another look, they would burst out laughing again.

Sadly, I was used to this by now and it hurt, but it was my normal and I continued counting down the Tube stops.

'Mum, it's our stop next.'

We stood up and I got off the Tube.

I turned, but Mum was still on the Tube, standing there talking to the OTT couple. Then she turned away and got off.

Mum stood next to me on the platform. The doors closed and she stared at the couple as the train left the station.

I looked at Mum and she had tears rolling down her cheeks. As she wiped them away, I felt so guilty, angry and embarrassed that Mum was crying. Somehow those tears were my fault.

This was new to me and it hit me so hard the more I realised my face affects the people close to me too. First my friend, and now my very first hero was hurt, and when I saw her in tears, it crushed me.

Why me? Why my mum? When is this going to get better?

That was one of my earliest memories of thinking that I needed to start hiding my face, or at least change people's focus.

Looking at the floor, avoiding eye contact, growing a long fringe and that bowl cut becoming even more ridiculous were now daily coping strategies.

Trying to avoid seeing my face. Avoiding the things that were causing me pain. No emotional outlets and a head full of dark, negative thoughts. I was lost.

What are your thoughts right now? What are your 'why me?' questions that are taking over your life and preventing you from thinking of the positives that you currently have?

I want you to try the following as it worked for me and I took a lot of comfort from it:

Think of a large space outside, get a sky lantern, write the why thoughts on it and then set it free in the big, open space and watch the whys float away. Or for a more environmentally friendly way, hold those same thoughts in your hand and wash them away in a stream of water – let's let them go.

And remember there's a difference between asking why and evaluating things and being obsessed with the whys – so final thought – don't stay with the 'whys' for too long.

So back to me. At 35 years old – 25 years after that incident on the Tube – one night I found a big, open space outside and I wrote on a sky lantern: 'Why did I have to look like this?'

I sat with those thoughts that I had all those years ago.

I lit it.

I watched it fill up with hot air.

And then I let it go.

I spent days, weeks, months, years asking 'why me?'

The question never went away.

I felt trapped by those two words.

Some time ago, I stopped asking 'why me?'

I don't know when, I don't know why, but I now realise that's the time I became free . . .

Free to love myself and the world around me. Through my experiences, through my observations.

I started to ask 'why me?' at such a young age.

People say that everything happens for a reason – I have said this many times too.

But there are things in my life that I wished I hadn't had to experience.

Yes, it's all made me who I am today, but it's because I've been able to do and continue to do the work on myself.

I'm lucky to be where I am today, through it all, but there's a part of me that wishes we didn't have a world that led to this innocent little child asking 'why me?'

I craved an answer that was impossible to find and it slowly ruined parts of my childhood and teenage years.

After we let go of the whys, we can then start to explore ourselves in a more rounded way, hopefully with a clearer mindset, open-hearted and ready for healing.

What feelings and emotions have you been hiding and are currently avoiding dealing with?

Why have you been avoiding or hiding them?

Is there something that is preventing you from sharing, dealing and beginning to work with them?

What do you need to support yourself from now on?

As we continue on this journey together, I will give you some guidance, but right now information-gathering is huge, and so is writing it all down. You may already be thinking and working out things that are going to support you going forward.

When things happen, we tend to want to move on quickly, or distract ourselves and do something to take our mind off of it, or we might immediately go and speak to someone about it but then try to forget it happened. But all this prevents us from feeling the feelings, listening to them, processing them, evaluating them and working them out. It's important to sit quietly with those feelings and acknowledge them.

Ignoring and hiding all my fears held me back for so many years, years that I won't ever get back. I missed out on life and memories because I hid away, scared and unable to do the work.

By not doing the work, I developed an anger and an attitude of *If people are going to stare, let's make it worth their while, let's entertain them and maybe they'll laugh with me instead of at me, maybe they'll like me if I please them.*

This again reminds us of the importance of self-love. We can only control our own actions, and how we behave and react to others. We also have the power to do the work on our own traumatic experiences. Other people's negativity and hate are not things for us to carry. They're extra emotional weight that we don't need. It's time to work on letting them go. That's the kind of weight we all can lose!

CHAPTER 3
IN TROUBLE, AGAIN?

The problem when you feel like you're the one at fault (even when you're not!) is that you start to feel frustrated and angry, and that inevitably comes out in your behaviour.

For me, the 'whys' started to change. I was avoiding the work that needed to be done, ignoring the root of my pain, and I put the blame on other things. I guess that's easier to do, as sometimes we don't know how to do the work and this affects our behaviour. I needed to work on loving myself and accepting what happened at my birth, but I didn't realise that then.

In my late teens my behaviour changed as I became filled with hate and anger, and I didn't talk to anyone about my thoughts or feelings.

That anger had nowhere to go, so it built up and festered inside me.

People tried to support me, but I had this poor attitude. I thought: *You don't know what it's like to be me, so how can you possibly help?* I lost the belief that anybody can become a hero and change your life for ever, or that any moment can, and I certainly wasn't able to be my own hero. If anything, I was turning into my very own villain, in self-destruct mode.

Looking back, I feel this – holding things in – was one of my biggest mistakes. People don't need to have experienced the same things that you've been through in life. It might help sometimes, but ultimately when people listen to you and you feel heard, it enables you to do some processing. It allows you to feel safe after you've shared something. This has been a game-changer in my adult life.

I had somehow developed into a bright, intelligent young lad. My friends would say that I wasn't the sharpest, but I was in all the top sets at school.

But with all these issues going on in my head, I soon became distracted.

I became the class clown, not caring about my grades.

I craved love, I wanted to be adored, but I felt so unattractive and unlovable that I went into survival mode. *How could I be loved and adored by others?*

During my final year at high school, I did anything I could to take the focus away from my face and the pain that it caused me. This was at a stage when I had let go of all my boundaries, just to be liked and accepted. I people-pleased, and I would do absolutely anything to feel something other than the pain I felt inside.

My education and grades no longer mattered to me. I had applied to college but didn't give it any real thought. I was focused on the now, and right now I needed attention, any attention other than on my face.

During an English class, my teacher went to fetch a pile of books that we were working through from the library.

My year group had just been to mainland Europe on a school trip. I didn't go – I never had the confidence to travel with my peers – but my friend had been and had purchased some fireworks. He brought them to school and knew exactly who would dare set light to one inside the classroom.

With a big, devious smile on his face, he looked at me and pulled one of these fireworks out.

It looked like a big crayon. He said all you had to do was strike the top, place it on the floor and it would give off sparks, fizzes and whizzes.

He was staring at me, his smile had widened and I knew exactly what he was about to say.

'Jono, I dare you to light this right now.'

Without any hesitation, and because the teacher had left us alone to get those books from the library, I grabbed the firework from him, stood up with a big smile on my face and went over to the front of the class. I struck the firework on the floor and placed it under the teacher's desk. Then I ran back to my seat as it began to spark up and explode.

The firework lit up the entire classroom and I just smiled.

The teacher came back in as the room began to fill up with smoke, and the neighbouring classes ran in to see what was going on.

'Get back to your classrooms!' the teacher yelled as he continued to walk into my firework display.

He stood for a moment amid all the smoke and scanned the classroom, looking for any clues as to who had done this.

He made his way to his desk and looked at the now dead firework. He paused.

Then with a calm voice he said, 'Does anyone want to share what happened?'

There was silence. Nobody was going to say anything, and he knew it.

He was defeated. Without another word about the firework, he asked someone to give each of us a book and told us all to read in silence for the remainder of the class.

As I read, all I could think was: *I can't wait till everyone finds out about this.* I didn't care what happened, or what the consequences were. I just wanted to entertain.

But as the school year went on, I soon felt some pressure to be even more extreme.

This pressure led to me getting my first tattoo. I discussed it with another friend, and we planned to hop on a bus to the neighbouring town and get one each.

In high school I was proper into rap, Biggie Smalls and Puff Daddy, so naturally I wanted a crucifix on my arm as they were in all the music videos, on chains and on their skin. I didn't want a small one either, I wanted it from shoulder to elbow.

The plan was that I would save my dinner money and eventually get one on my lunch break.

Mum would give me £5 per day for lunch. I bought a beetroot and mayonnaise sandwich, which cost 35p and meant I saved £4.65 per day, depending on whether I managed not to buy anything else.

After a month of beetroot and mayonnaise sandwiches, I had enough money saved up. So, with all my pound coins, I headed to town with my friend to get my very first tattoo.

We showed up at the studio with our passports to prove our age and he was happy to permanently ink our young, untouched skin.

'Go choose one, mate,' he said.

I scrolled through the books and the boards and after a few minutes I found a crucifix that I liked and said, 'I'll have that one, please.'

'Where do you want it, pal?'

I flexed my right arm and said, 'Here, please.'

I'd been doing a few bicep curls throughout the month, so my flex game was on point!

He applied the transfer and asked me to go and look in the mirror to see if I was happy with it.

As always, I looked at the mirror, avoiding my face, and as I saw my arm I smiled and said, 'Yeah, I'm happy with that.'

He sat me in his chair and proceeded to ink a red-brown tribal crucifix on my arm, while eating a cheeseburger. Yes, man's gotta eat.

As he permanently inked my pure skin, I felt so cold and sick. My whole arm shook, it hurt that much. I've had a lot of tattoos since and they've never felt like that. Obviously 16-year-old Jonathan was totally unprepared and too young for this.

Once he was finished, he cleaned me up, wiping away the leftover ink and blood. It stung. I walked over to the mirror and I got to see it for the first time. I wasn't impressed. I didn't like it. There was instant regret.

'That's £40, mate,' he said.

I handed him my money, thanked him and thought: *Maybe it will get better in time.*

We went back to school and of course everyone wanted to see. Reluctantly I showed them. There was no 'That's cool, mate, that's sick.'

People saw it and were like, 'Mate, you got a tattoo.'

I hated it. Everyone went to class and I felt so alone. I instantly slipped back into that thought process: *This wouldn't have happened if I didn't look like this. If my birth parents hadn't left me, I wouldn't have done this.* I hid for the rest of the school day as I didn't want to show anyone.

At home, I stared at my tattoo for hours in the mirror, praying that it would look better.

It didn't.

Instead, it scabbed heavily, and at home I had to cover it up 24/7 as I was scared to show my mum.

But on a positive note, there were no more beetroot sandwiches for a while!

Soon my entire identity became centred around trauma and pity. It was all I knew.

I started to lie to make things sound worse.

I remember watching a film where kids at school sold cocaine, and they stored it in pens after emptying the ink tube.

So I thought: *That's what I can do next.*

I wasn't a drug lord, but I was creative.

At home, alone, I went into the kitchen and gathered all the white powder-like substances I could: sugar, salt, washing powder. I mixed them up, grabbed my empty pen and snorted it.

My nose bled. I tried again and it burned my nose. It was too obvious that it wasn't real. It burned, it was sweet and smelled of flowers.

So I needed to get even more creative. I found some tablets and crushed them up with flour. It needed to be more consistent, so I got my ruler out and crushed them even more. I snorted it through my pen and was happy with that.

I loaded several pens and placed them in my pencil case and took them to school. I didn't have a plan at this point for what I was going to do with them. It was just the next 'Look at me' moment.

During science class, I was talking to my friend and got one of my loaded pens out, making sure he saw it. His face was a picture of awe and curiosity. I didn't say anything and went to the toilet. In fear of making my nose bleed, I emptied it down the toilet and returned to class. My friend looked at me and just smiled.

I fed off that smile. Job done!

At 3.30pm I walked home. To avoid the double-decker buses, I preferred to walk home on my own as fast as I could, but my friend who had seen the pen ran to catch up with me.

'Jono, what's in the pens? Can I have one?'

I replied, 'I don't know what's really in them. I got them from someone.' Of course it was all lies; I knew exactly what the ingredients were – crushed Paracetamol, Ibuprofen, Ritalin and a little bit of flour! (Self-raising flour if you were wondering.)

But I took off my rucksack, reached in and pulled out two loaded pens from my pencil case, and now, with added peer pressure, I had to snort the contents again. With my friend looking on, I put the pen up my nose and snorted, and – you got it – my nose bled. My friend held back from doing his, he just put the pen in his pocket and walked alongside me as I continued to pinch my bloody nose.

Whenever I got into trouble, when I realised I had done wrong or made a bad decision (I was currently making them daily), again I reflected on the 'whys':

Why am I doing this?

Why am I like this?

And every time my answer was: *It wouldn't be like this if my birth parents hadn't left me, and I wouldn't be dealing with this if my face looked like everyone else's.*

The fact is I got into trouble because of my poor attitude and behaviour, but I blamed it all on my face and my situation, and that was way off the mark.

The more I blamed my face and my situation, the

59

longer it took for me to heal. In fact, I wasn't healing, I was creating even more trauma and getting further and further away from any kind of self-love.

I was spiralling out of control. I had no boundaries, and I was constantly trying to people-please. I didn't care about my grades, my health, my wellbeing or those around me. I just wanted attention!

I thought I needed to people-please for people to want to be associated with me. I needed to people-please to be liked, to be invited, to be included and, hopefully, to be loved.

This was a scary precedent that I was setting for myself. People-pleasing with no boundaries would come to bite me in the butt big time later down the line.

As an adult, one of the biggest things I've learned is setting boundaries, and it's taken me till my thirties to properly get there. Actually, it's still a work in progress. Certain people and situations can challenge your boundaries – deliberately or accidentally, may I add – but I now set boundaries in all aspects of my life. There are still moments when I feel bad, even guilty, for putting a boundary in place with someone. But I realise that I need to keep myself safe and if people don't respect that then they are not good for me.

When I'm with friends, we have the same sense of humour and they still dare me to do things. I don't ever want to lose that humour, but I can now better navigate what to do and what not to do.

I know my worth, my value, and what I bring to the table, and that's not dares or drama: I bring my epic, unique energy and that's why people want to be around me, that's why I am loved and invited to be part of this friendship group. I'm empowered to do things for me and when something isn't good for me, I know I have the power to say no. (Although I'm still working on this, and I do occasionally feel guilty when I say no.)

As I was writing this book, I went through a break-up. All break-ups suck. It was a relationship that was going really well, I turned up as my authentic self and attracted someone pretty amazing, but eventually she walked away, it wasn't for her. When she called it off, she asked if we could still be friends. She really wanted that and in the past, even though I was hurting, I would have taken that pain and been that friend.

But this time I looked at her and said, 'No, I can't do that right now.' It hurt so much, I felt so guilty, but I knew what boundaries would keep me emotionally safe. She left. It was so hard to do, but that week I felt a small sense of pride that, despite the pain, I had done something to keep myself safe. I learned a few valuable things from this break-up, but more on that later.

Boundaries come in the workplace too. How many

times have you taken work home? Worked on days off? Neglected your time to fit other people's needs in? Neglected your needs and safety to please others?

It's all to do with boundary-setting, and the more you do it, the healthier you will feel – and your friends and loved ones will always respect and support those boundaries.

How is your boundary-setting?

Do you know what your boundaries are and how others need to respect them?

Typically we have seven different areas where we need to set boundaries:

- Physical
- Sexual
- Emotional/mental
- Spiritual/religious
- Financial
- Time
- Non-negotiable boundaries

What are your boundaries in each area?

Does poor boundary-setting lead you into situations that you'd rather not be in?

Do you wish that you'd said no at an early stage but then it was too late and you found yourself doing something you didn't want to be doing?

This is something that I still have to work on. But, like me, give it a try. Stand your ground and do it for *you*!

While doing this task, please consider other people's boundaries too.

CHAPTER 4
SOMEONE IS BETTER
THAN NO ONE?

Have you ever felt everyone around you was all loved up?
That all you see when you go out is cute couples holding
hands? People announcing engagements and pregnancies
on social media? And you're jealous and can't help but
think: *I want that*.

For me, from the ages of 15 to 18 it felt like I saw that
everywhere I went. It felt like all my friends were getting
into relationships. I saw them hooking up at parties and
then holding hands at school. Naturally I wanted to
experience that too, but at parties when we played Spin
the Bottle, when I joined in everyone else left. No one
wanted to kiss me and certainly nobody wanted to go out

with me. I tried and tried but never had any luck. Looking back as an adult, I don't blame anyone and I don't think anyone did anything wrong to me. We were all young and trying to find our way through life.

But the obsession with 'why' transferred to an obsession with being wanted by another. I felt so incomplete that I hadn't experienced a girlfriend or that I had never been kissed, or told that someone fancied me. I craved this affection more than anything at that point.

However, since you're here reading this book . . .

If you have a young person in your life, it would be a great idea to discuss games like Spin the Bottle, and others like it, before they attend their first party. When they get to that age, say 12 or 13, you can advise them that these games exist. It's the perfect time to introduce concepts of consent and bodily autonomy, and, dare I say, kindness and empathy.

You could introduce these topics, and if they haven't run from the room screaming yet, ask 'What would you do if no one wanted to kiss you?' Or 'How would you handle it if you got the "gross" person?' More than prescribing or controlling an interaction, these conversations equip them to question the point of these games and their participation in them.

Looking back, I wish I had been bold enough to say I did not want to play, or someone had been kind enough if their spin had landed on me to say, 'I'm not ready to kiss. Is a high five cool?'

Of course it's not cool, but the confidence and courage to own the moment will leave you looking like a rock star and avoiding years of potential regret.

So, the kissing games were PG. The next part was truly life-altering – alcohol, the social lubricant that can quickly cause a young person to slide into depression or addiction.

I remember being invited to my very first weekend party. By the time year 10 had arrived, I was very settled and had a great friendship group. I had my struggles, but I was still in the top sets, just about getting by in exams and home-work. I would meet my friends after school and we would play football till it got dark, despite the demons in my head. As I say, I was getting by.

We were lined up to go into class one day and everyone was talking about a party at the weekend. I listened in, curious as to what they were on about, and my friend cas-ually turned to me and asked if I was going.

I said that I hadn't been invited.

He was like, 'Shut up, everyone's invited, you're coming!'

As excited as I was, I was equally terrified.

Luckily my friend whom I gave the contents of the pen

to was sat next to me in class and he was invited too. He had been to a few before so I spent the entire lesson quizzing him about all these parties.

'What goes on?'

'What do I wear?'

'What should I drink?'

'What time does everyone get there?'

'What do you tell your parents?'

'Who else goes?'

I needed to know everything!

He was so chill about it all.

He said he had been to loads and that they were ace. Everyone just got drunk and had a laugh.

He said he would meet me beforehand and take me somewhere to buy alcohol, and then we would head to the party together.

All I needed to do was wear something nice and tell my mum I was sleeping at his house.

So that's what I did.

I wore my best clothes – baggy cargo trousers, a pair of Kickers and a silk zip-up shirt from Topman – and as for my hair, you guessed it, I went to the bathroom and tidied up my bowl cut!

I soaked myself with Lynx Africa and headed out to meet my friend.

So far so good.

We walked to a small shop. My friend said, 'This is the place we get all our alcohol from. Don't say anything, just follow me in.'

There were other customers inside, so my friend said, 'Just look at the sweets until they leave.'

They soon left and then the lady behind the counter closed the shop door and locked it. She went back behind her counter and asked us what we wanted.

I hadn't even thought about this properly.

I froze.

She was staring at me, waiting for me to reply.

I looked behind her and saw all the spirits.

'Have you decided yet?'

I was trying to decide what I wanted and figure out what I could afford.

I scanned all the bottles and clocked a bottle of Teacher's whisky in my price range.

'I'll take a bottle of Teacher's whisky,' I said.

She looked at me for a moment and didn't respond.

I was like: *Oh no, have I said the wrong thing?*

She still hadn't responded, so I said: 'Please.'

She turned and grabbed the bottle and asked, 'How many of you will be drinking this?'

'A few of us,' I said.

She grabbed a bag, put the bottle inside and handed it to me.

Her final words to me were: 'That's strong stuff. Be careful.'

I nodded, took it from her and left the shop.

My friend was smiling and had chosen a few cans of Special Brew.

Clutching our drinks, we headed to the house party.

My friend didn't even knock on the door and just walked in.

It's mad but one of the things that stuck with me from entering this house was the door; it was the first time I had seen a white PVC door and I thought it was so posh and fancy with its delicate glass patterns and skinny keyhole. The door handles even went up and down when you opened or locked the door. My house door was made of wood and had a massive piece of frosted glass in the middle. The door handle only went down and our house key was like a massive skeleton key that you would typically associate with opening the door to a dungeon.

Anyways, we went through this posh, fancy door and I was at my first fucking house party.

Everyone I knew was there!

It was so amazing to see all my friends together outside of school in a party setting, just having such a laugh.

I'd only seen this in movies or heard a few people talk about what had happened at previous parties at school. But here I was, and it was the coolest and scariest thing ever.

I was so nervous that I held on to my bottle of whisky tightly. It was the only thing that I felt was under my control. I just didn't know where to go or what to do. I think a part of me really wanted to run back home.

I saw a few of my friends playing on a PlayStation in the corner, so I headed over to them and watched as they all competed for the fastest lap time around a circuit on *Gran Turismo*.

It was weird. I knew all these people, but I was scared. It was like I'd forgotten how to speak or make conversation. In fact, today I still feel socially awkward around larger groups of people.

I remember somebody finding a little device where you stuck patches on to your muscles, and when you turned the device on it would send a small electrical current into your muscles that made them pulse.

A few people tried it, and when it shocked them everyone laughed at their reaction.

I really wanted to be a part of this party, so I asked them to attach the device to me.

My friends were more than willing, so I rolled up my

shirt sleeve and offered my arm – yes, the one with the shit tattoo on it – and I watched them put the patches on and let them shock me.

It didn't hurt but made my arm jolt.

I said, 'You can turn it up higher if you want.'

My friends didn't need a second invitation, so they turned it up higher and shocked me again and again.

Everyone started to watch to see how far I dared go, and as it began to hurt I couldn't stop because I was a part of something. This was my admission to the party.

I think the novelty eventually wore off and people soon disappeared to get more drinks and enjoy other aspects of the party. My friends pulled the stickers off me, said that I was ace and then I just sat there and watched everyone mingle.

I'm not sure how much time had gone by, but I hadn't even opened my bottle. I was still clinging to it for dear life.

The friend I'd arrived with found me and asked if he could have a shot of my whisky. He was surprised that I hadn't opened it.

He took it off me, opened it, poured himself some into the bottle top and drank it like a shot. Then, without even asking me, he poured another and handed it to me. I drank, and it was possibly the worst thing that I had ever tasted. It burned.

But then others came over because they had seen the whisky.

'Where've you been hiding that then?' they said.

The attention was back on me again, along with the pressure to do something to be seen.

A few people took it in turns to do shots and as they did everyone cheered, but then they started to disappear just like before.

I felt an emptiness in my stomach, and I didn't want them to leave me. So I jumped up and yelled, 'Hey, guys, watch this!'

As they turned and gathered around me, I downed that bottle of whisky till it was empty. That was it for me that night. I don't remember any of the rest.

The following Monday back at school, I was eager to know what had happened at the party, I wanted to hear all the stories. My friends shared who pulled who and my heart sank, I didn't pull, then they laughed and said that I'd downed the whisky like a madman and passed out and every now and again people would take me for a walk around the garden to make sure I was OK.

Hearing these conversations and being a part of the stories, alongside my friends that I looked up to, was such a massive thing for me. I wanted to be in all their stories and the only way I felt that I could make this happen was to continue to do these stupid things.

Some of my friends recognised that about my behaviour, and they would pull me to one side and tell me I was one of the boys and I didn't need to do all these stupid things. They were all my heroes, and I couldn't thank them enough for being my friends, so in a way this was also me repaying them.

Thank you for being my friend, I must repay you by being stupid!

We would drink on the weekends, and more heavily at these parties that were held less often. Before every party started, I trimmed my shit bowl cut, wore my best clothes and turned up as the best-packaged version of myself I felt I could create.

The parties were where I wanted to be, but then I needed to survive and get through them with as little pain as possible. The first hour was always OK because it was just fun and great to be around everyone. But as the night wore on and the looser people got, the more intoxicated I became. The dark thoughts started to creep in: *Can anyone see me? Would anyone care if I wasn't here?* Then, of course, towards the end of the party people started to couple up, which crushed me. I felt so alone and unseen, and eventually turned to the whisky. My party trick.

On Sunday mornings, I felt so low and depressed. I had no drive, no get up and go, like my soul just wasn't there any more.

I thought about my birth parents. There's a saying that goes 'He's got a face that only a mother could love', but my mother couldn't love my face and if even my parents couldn't love me, if they couldn't stick around, how was anyone else going to be able to do that? I had found an incredible, loving forever family, but I couldn't shift these feelings. In fact, endings, goodbyes and separations are still things I struggle with and I either find myself staying in situations too long or unable to cope with endings. If I feel someone pull away I love them even more because I don't want to be left again. I remember as a child, when me and Mum had visitors, when it came to the goodbyes, we would always stand out at the gate and wave them off. Every time I stood there and waved, my tummy would flip and I never knew why. Nothing bad had happened but I felt a sadness from a simple goodbye. This continued to happen in adulthood and I think it adds to the pain when I face a break-up.

Alcohol does not do any of us favours in this area. A friend of mine describes the fall-out as a social-anxiety hangover or, to use a more common term, 'hangxiety'. And it turns out there's a reason for the depressive, anxiety-inducing effects of alcohol after the first burst of false confidence it gives us has disappeared.

The body has a series of systems that work together – from the nerves that run throughout the body to the tiny cells that defend us against harmful substances. An

NOT ALL HEROES WEAR CAPES

essential part of all of these systems is the neurotransmitter called gamma-aminobutyric acid (GABA).*

GABA regulates the nervous system, which is responsible for the body's balance, ability to move, thought processes, alertness, the five senses and so on. GABA also has a calming effect and can block signals from your central nervous system, so normally it helps decrease anxiety and other mental health symptoms. But GABA can't properly function under certain circumstances, such as excessive drinking. Studies show that alcohol depletes the production of GABA, causing side effects that can lead to physical, emotional and mental health damage. It's one of the reasons why, despite how good you may feel on a night out, you sometimes wake up feeling anxious, self-conscious or regretful, even if you didn't do anything embarrassing the night before!

Anyway, back to my story. I left high school, and the sadness I felt was huge; saying goodbye to the people and places that made up my safety net knocked me. The next was unknown and it terrified me.

I started college and began to drink even more to get by.

* Georgetown Behavioral Hospital, 'GABA and Alcohol: How Drinking Leads to Anxiety'. https://www.gbhoh.com/gaba-and-alcohol-how-drinking-leads-to-anxiety/.

My social anxiety was at an all-time high. So, depleted, dehydrated and desperate, I'd find myself in my Sunday morning feels. I couldn't bear to be alone in that state and, desperate to feel a connection with someone, I would grab my mobile, make up phone numbers and just dial. Taking an existing number and changing the last two digits often worked.

This also created a dependency on having a mobile with credit on it. We had pay-as-you-go mobiles back then – contracts weren't really a thing – so I went back to the beetroot and mayo sandwiches to ensure I always had enough phone credit.

With a fully loaded pay-as-you-go mobile, I would ring these random numbers. If a guy answered I would say, 'Sorry, I've dialled the wrong number,' and hang up.

If a girl answered, I would ask for my friend and they would be like, 'You've got the wrong number.'

I'd apologise and then hang up. Moments later, I would text them asking them where their accent was from as it sounded unusual. And yes, I'm very aware of that sounding creepy and very selfish right now, but at 17 years old I craved a connection and didn't think of anything other than my own needs.

This didn't go anywhere, and despite well over a hundred attempts over a few weekends, there were no replies or responses.

Then, one day, my phone beeped. I'd received a reply to one of my messages.

The text from this stranger simply said, 'I'm from London. Where are you from?'

I replied, 'I'm from West Yorkshire.'

I don't remember how the conversation went on from there, but within two weeks we were talking and I had planned a trip down south to see her.

There were no picture messages back then, so I posted her some photos of my friend, stating that it was me. I was too embarrassed to share a photo of myself. She wouldn't want to meet the real me. I fed her so many lies to try to sell a better version of myself. If she had any likes, I liked them too. I thought maybe if I got to see her, she'd give me a chance.

I didn't care about the risks or dangers I was taking. I lied to my mum and said that I was staying at a friend's house. Then I caught a bus that took six hours to reach London and then a train that took another two hours to reach her village. Nobody had a clue where I was and, in truth, I didn't know this person, their story or even what their motive was. She had just replied to a random call from me. *I'm from London.* I was that desperate, they could have literally written anything in that text and I would have ended up in this situation, hundreds of miles from home with no one knowing where I was or who I was with.

So, nobody knew where I was, as I sat in that train carriage holding some flowers I'd picked up before boarding, heading to a place I'd never been to. Station after station went by and I found myself further and further away from home but getting closer and closer to a stranger I'd known only two weeks. The train announced the name of the next station and that was my stop. I was about to meet her, hoping she was there. Safety wasn't even a concern, I just needed a person.

The train slowly came to a stop. It was dark by then. I put on my coat, grabbed my bag and stepped off the train with the flowers.

My phone rang. It was her. I was the only person on the platform and she'd asked, 'Where are you?' I awkwardly looked at her across the station and waved and said, 'It's me.'

I was so scared. I wanted to get back on the train but it was too late. The doors had closed and the train was on the move. I felt sick but I started to move my feet and I found myself walking towards her. I didn't look at her as I gave her the flowers. We barely spoke as we walked to her dad's car. We got in and I found myself in a stranger's car heading to an unknown place. I had no control at this point. He drove us to their house, while I stared out of the window the whole time, not knowing what to do next. I hadn't planned this far.

He pulled up outside the house and got out. I got out of the car and just followed them inside. I entered the house and met the family, who luckily were all polite and welcoming. After some brief, very awkward, uncomfortable introductions, we went to her room.

She then stood in front of me and repeatedly said, 'Look at me.' I could hear what she was saying but I just looked down at the floor.

'Look at me.'

She pulled my face up to look at her.

'Why didn't you tell me? Why didn't you say anything?'

I shared that I was scared that if I had shown her my face, she wouldn't have wanted to meet me.

She looked at me, she kissed me, and later that night I had sex for the first time.

A day that could have gone very wrong actually led to one of the best days of my teenage life – somehow I had found someone that looked at me and, despite my differences, found me sexually attractive, which was huge for me back then.

Out of respect to the other person, I'm not going into much more detail about this relationship. I was 17 and this was the start of a very unhealthy relationship for me that led me to do a lot of things I didn't want to do, both emotionally and sexually. I was never forced into doing these things, but emotionally – I felt I had to do all kinds of things that I didn't want to do to maintain the relationship. I was all in, at any cost.

This was my first relationship and I found it very hard to navigate through. I was scared of doing anything that would lead to the end of the relationship so I gave and gave with no boundaries and a people-pleasing mindset, even at times when I knew deep down I should have taken a step back. But I still think of all the ways it could have been even worse. That kind of desperation has resulted in dire consequences for some people. It sets up a life of trauma and regret. I cannot stress enough how deeply depressed I was at such a young age that I literally didn't care if terrible things happened to me.

Luckily this relationship, although challenging, did have some happier moments and hasn't left me with any lifelong trauma or regret. It just gave me my first lesson in love and relationships – be in it with shared boundaries and respect for one another.

I say this so you can understand that warning children in a similar situation – or, worse, threatening them – is not a viable option. When someone is in this kind of pain, tragedy seems almost welcome. It's an escape from their current unbearable feelings.

At 17, and as a young man who yearned to

people-please, regardless of boundaries, I deeply needed to feel a connection.

I was so desperately giving.

In her own way my partner kept me safe and I feel that she did love me. But during this time, I spent all my savings and chose to do things that hurt me; I put myself in situations where I felt jealous, and as a teenager, how do you deal with that? I soaked it all up and just sat with it, by myself, trying to keep it together, hoping that this relationship would continue – that we would stay together.

Despite what I was going through, I now thought I was like everyone else: I had a person that found me sexually attractive, and that was all that mattered to me then. This went on for months, and then the relationship ended. It crushed me. At the time I had lost the only thing that made me feel complete. I relied on this person so much I don't think I would have ever called it off no matter how I was feeling.

Thinking back on this years later, the one big thing I took away from this relationship was that I depended too much on the relationship, on another human being, to feel complete, to feel accepted, to feel loved, to feel that I belonged to something. Even though it wasn't right for me, like a drug, I needed it and when it ended – it felt like I had nothing worth living for, and that was scary.

I had no love or respect for myself back then, so if I met

someone that showed me even one per cent effort and shared one per cent of their love, that would have felt like enough for me. I felt this was my level and I accepted it.

Being so devastated after our break-up, I found new lows and sank even more into the darkness of the world.

I hid away with all my thoughts. There was no bliss; I felt everything negatively and I didn't want to feel anything any more. I wanted my life to end.

By the time I was 18 or 19 years old, I would drink and go out with all my friends, the same ones from school, the same ones that showed me love and reminded me daily I was one of the boys, but I was on this unhealthy quest to try and find another person. I needed to feel attractive again. It never happened. These nights followed the same pattern as my school parties: the first hour or so was fun, I'm out with the boys, but soon it became a toxic, dark place for me, with people meeting, mixing, laughing and enjoying life while I felt like an extra in a movie watching the lead characters hook up. I enviously watched it all happening from the sidelines; I just couldn't compete. I didn't belong there. Despite giving every part of myself away, I wasn't good enough. I wasn't seen. I felt like I wasn't there.

I eventually met a girl during this time, and started seeing her – she was another person who, like me, was dealing with a lot of trauma. She stayed in temporary emergency accommodation and had a history of drug use.

One night I went to see her at this hostel she was staying at and someone overdosed. As the person lay on the ground, people were just stood over them, not quite sure what to do. There were tears, shouting, arguing, blame. I rang 999 for help.

That night scared me. I left alone and headed home.

I still lived with my mum, and she still slept on the sofa downstairs and would always ask me how my night had gone.

I told her nothing.

Days passed and I had not heard from the girl that I was seeing. I rang and rang but got no response. Eventually, I went back to the hostel in the hope of seeing her. I knocked on the door and a familiar face answered.

'Jono, she doesn't live here any more.'

They explained that she was well, but had been rehomed somewhere else and they had no contact details for her. I took it as another loss. Another one had left me and, no matter what I did, I was unable to prevent people from leaving me.

I often think where my life would have taken me if she had answered that day. Would we have reconnected? I still had no boundaries . . . What dark, desperate path for connection would I have gone down?

I was so close to drugs and still don't fully understand how I made it out of that place without trying any. I realise how unfair this may seem to some of you. Maybe you know someone who overdosed. Why did I avoid falling prey to drugs, but they didn't? I can't answer that. All I know is that my heart has been in the darkness. The great Pema Chödrön once wrote:

> Compassion is not a relationship between the healer and the wounded. It's a relationship between equals. Only when we know our own darkness well can we be present with the darkness of others. Compassion becomes real when we recognise our shared humanity.*

Experiencing these dark places, by being vulnerable and open about them, has enabled me to connect with so many people across the world, across diagnoses, across language barriers. It doesn't make me better. I'm only their equal – your equal.

The more self-love that I have developed over the years, the more people I have attracted, in all kinds of ways, and I recognise more than ever what is good for me and what is not.

That other person that you're romantically invested in,

---

* Pema Chödrön, *The Places That Scare You: A Guide to Fearlessness in Difficult Times.*

that person beside yourself, is one of the biggest emotional investments you can make in life – don't ever settle for just anyone!

With all this in mind, let's take a look at your current relationships with family members, friends, lovers and work colleagues. I want you to ask yourself this: are they healthy relationships?

I'm sure many of them are. But are there any where you are letting the person sap parts of your energy, your worth? Are there any where your boundaries aren't respected?

We now know from the last chapter where our boundaries lie. If we set them in place in our current relationships, who would respect them?

I know how hard it can be to let go of people, but you do need the right people in your circle.

CHAPTER 5
DOES ANYBODY EVEN CARE?

With all the stages that come and go throughout our lives, I'm sure you've wondered at times: *What's the point of doing this?* You may have thought that nobody actually cares what happens to you. *Why do I even bother?*

Even when we've done the work, are feeling confident and have been our authentic self, we can still have these feelings.

I went through this phase in my life when I felt I wasn't seen and that nobody cared. When I'm going through struggles I can still slip back into these negative thoughts.

There was a period when, out of nowhere, I started to miss my biologicial dad. All my friends seemed to have dads. I didn't know whether they were positive role models or not – I just assumed they were – but I would see them on the school run, or out at the weekends, or just overhear conversations. 'Me and my dad did this yesterday.' 'My dad says that when you're with a girl you need to do this.'

I absolutely love that I was brought up by a single mum, an older single mum in fact, because it's given me a lot of great qualities and made me become someone who feels. I was brought up to cry and have conversations that were hard. I had lost that skill by this point in my life, but it was still present somewhere deep inside me.

But when I was out and about and I saw a father and son moment, I felt sad. I craved what I believed a father would bring: he'd drive a car (my mum didn't), he would help me find a girlfriend, he would teach me how to score a goal round the back of the house and he would definitely make sure I went to the hairdresser's.

I had distant thoughts that maybe, one day, when I had a family of my own, I could be the father I never had. That motivated me, but instantly that motivation was lost as the thought *Nobody would ever want to have kids with me* took over.

In my teenage years, I learned that my condition (Treacher Collins syndrome) has a 50/50 chance of being passed on to any children I may have, and as I got older this fact played on my mind so much.

I now had to find someone who would, along with finding me attractive, also be OK supporting me with this. I was emotionally tormented before it had even happened.

I thought, *Surely this imaginary father figure would be able to give me the best advice on this.*

I had grown up with children in the house 24/7 and I love kids. I'm still a big kid, to be honest, so I saw having children in my future – a little blue-eyed Jonathan running around, taking off his hearing aid when I was talking to him. Those thoughts made me smile.

But then what about the health risks and all the pain that comes with Treacher Collins?

If I ever met a girl who liked me, when would I tell her? When we first met, being transparent and letting her know what would be in store for her? If I did that, surely she would run a mile!

But, what if I didn't tell her and she somehow fell in love with me and I only told her then? That wouldn't be fair either.

As a teenager I was having this internal battle that wasn't even something I had to deal with right then, but, as before, I became obsessed with it. Somehow my thought process was: *One day I'll have a vasectomy and I won't have to worry about it.* That was my childlike answer to the problem.

There was a war going on inside me. I pushed away all the allies I had in my life and kept them out, believing a phantom, father-like person was the answer.

Drink clouded my thoughts and made me even more depressed and conflicted.

Why does nobody care about me?

People did, people do, but because I wasn't getting answers immediately, because my happiness wasn't found immediately, I didn't feel or connect with all the things that I was blessed to have, and I had a lot.

As I got older, I started going to clubs with my friends. I found them to be the most humiliating places. I would get dressed the best I could, I would style and preen the best I could, I would drink before I went out, but I'd still feel sick and anxious.

I always met my friends in town – I somehow felt safer that way. But as soon as I arrived, I would head to the toilet in panic and try to settle my anxiety. I'd check my outfit in the mirror to make sure there was nothing to critique. (Though, saying that, if you ask my friends they'd say my fashion sense was always risky.)

Those trips to the toilet became more frequent throughout the night and I began to hide.

When I was not hiding away, I would be around my friends, looking at the floor, scared to make eye contact with anyone. Scared to interact, scared to make a fool of myself, scared to be seen, scared to ruin my friends' night.

My friends loved me and if they saw anyone being unkind to me, they would always step in. But I didn't want that. I never wanted to be in a situation where they had to step in for me. I was so lucky to have them, but it was embarrassing when it happened. They would always invite me on holidays but I said no every time, for that reason: people would be unkind, my friends would step in and defend me, they'd fight and I would ruin their holiday.

Back in the club, on the dance floor, I felt everyone mixing with others around them, vibing and connecting with the world around them. I just craved a connection with someone.

On nights out, there was always that banger towards the end of the night that would bring us all together for one final dance. It would start to play and all of a sudden all my friends would appear with a massive grin on their faces: arms in the air, hugging and singing together in one giant circle. For a moment, I'm part of it, together with my friends, connected by a song.

I particularly remember a more upbeat, dance version of a John Denver song with the lyrics 'Country roads take me home / To the place where I belong'. It would get faster and then slower, louder and quieter. We would sing at the top of our lungs.

But gradually, the song played out, and I'd watch my friends leave, some with partners, others with people they'd met during the night and some heading to the takeaway. It felt like a goodbye and my tummy would get tied up in knots again. This aspect of going to the club soon became the worst part of the evening for me. The music had stopped, the places to hide had gone and I'd find myself in a takeaway full of bright lights, or in a queue with bored, drunk people. 'Last chance to pull,' my friends joked.

I hated these places. Nobody cared that I was there, nobody cared if I left. So I would. I would leave and walk off on my own.

But the truth is that I had made it like that. People did care. I had just lost the ability to ask for help when I needed it most.

It's around a three-mile walk from town to my house, and I walked alone, with the darkest of thoughts going through my head.

I walked through the town. The houses gradually stopped as I eventually came to a stretch of road between fields and a crematorium, which was where the final road that took me from town to my local village was. The road starts high and goes down into a dip when you reach the crematorium. I was always scared to walk by the crematorium, so I tended to walk in the middle of the road.

One night when I was walking in the road, a taxi came whizzing over the hill and nearly hit me. Luckily, I managed to rush over to the path, but my heart was racing, my knees going weak as it dawned on me that the taxi had nearly hit me.

I stood there and I cried. I felt pain. I wished that taxi had hit me.

I looked around me. I looked for hope, but all I could see was that long country road ahead of me.

I remembered the John Denver song:

Country roads, take me home
To the place I belong . . .

I felt like I didn't belong in this world, obsessed with image and looks. I wanted to go to the place where I belonged.

I didn't know where that was, though. I didn't have one. I didn't have a safe place. I've never tried to take my own life, but after that moment I hoped I would be involved in a tragic accident that ended it all for me.

It's a selfish thought, but there have been times that I've hoped the plane I was on wouldn't make it across the ocean; I've walked down roads that I knew were danger-ous, hoping that I would meet the wrong person at the wrong time; I've prayed and wished for things that I'm embarrassed to admit because people face that heartache of losing someone this way, and it's life-changing for them and so many people around them. But I just wanted my life to end.

Step by step, I continued to walk home, the thoughts

reinforced with every step I took. The streetlights lit the way, the odd taxi passed me. All the houses were quiet and there wasn't a soul in sight.

Would anybody actually miss me if I wasn't here?

As I got close to my house, I composed myself. I couldn't let anyone see me like that, especially my mum.

I entered the house and snuck upstairs. I climbed into bed, took my hearing aid off and closed my eyes with those new thoughts in my head.

Are you ready to go a little deeper?

Let me ask you this: what are the scariest thoughts that you have in your head right now, the ones you're scared to admit?

And this one's a tough one to answer, but I'm asking you this because I have been asked it and being able to speak about it was really helpful for me:

Have you ever had suicidal thoughts or thoughts about dying?

Do you know you are not alone in feeling like this?

I have had suicidal thoughts and at times often thought about dying.

Do you know that there are people who do care about you and that there are so many people out there who are willing to listen to and support you?

It's so important to find someone you can talk to, no matter how dark your thoughts. A friend, or sometimes a stranger, can just listen while you talk about how you're feeling, and it's a huge relief to open up to them.

At the back of the book there are several resources for you to reach out to now.

You are not alone! I will be sharing more personal experiences of this later in the book.

Remember, we're in this together.

I'm pretty certain all of us have scary thoughts that enter our mind, and we choose to either ignore them or just pray and hope that they will pass.

But what happens if they don't pass? What happens if they consume you until you reach a point of no return?

Please get that stuff out of your head.

In 2021, I set myself the challenge of finding something that I loved about myself every single day and I posted it, sharing it to my social media profiles so that I had it documented for future reference. Sometimes it was hard. I found it was like exercise. I needed rest days and I needed to listen to my feelings, but in the end I found 170 things I loved about myself.

During the year I revisited every area of my life: the good, the bad, the painful. I even did that three-mile walk again at 3am, past the crematorium, down into my village. As I walked it this time, I felt how much I had grown.

As I was doing this I read over my adoption reports, which I'm lucky to have. I have around 15 of them that record the people who met to discuss my situation and my future.

At the top of every sheet of paper it starts with the date, time and location. Underneath that is a list of names of the six people who attended each meeting about me.

I don't know these people, but what I do know is that I had nothing I could offer them – neither money nor even a thank you – but they fought for me and my future.

You may not see it, but people do care about you and you will feel it eventually. Please remember that.

Have a think about who's checked in on you recently – who's called, who's texted?

Who's tried to make plans with you? Who's given you that smile that says 'I've got you'?

When was the last time you called or reached out to someone too? It's a two-way thing. I'm sure you have so many people who would be there if you reached out, and the only reason they are not is because you've not asked for help!

> We get so lost in our heads, we often miss these opportunities for people to help us or reassure us that they're there for us.

Throughout my entire life I've been loved!

Even when I've not seen, felt or even understood it, people have loved me, even in the hardest of places.

So, I wanted to share some massive love and respect to my 'secret' badass grandma.

When I was given up for adoption, people from my birth family tried to maintain contact and my maternal grandma was one of them. She made contact with me without telling her family (my birth family). She did it all in secret so no one would get hurt while she tried to build a relationship with me.

As a child, I thought having a secret grandma was such a cool thing.

I wasn't allowed to phone or write to her, but every now and again I got these beautiful handwritten letters, and then my mum and I would arrange these secret meetings with her.

We would meet in town for a drink and some food.

On birthdays and at Christmas, she would send cards along with a £5 note to spend on what I liked. She even bought me my very first England football shirt.

As a child, this was the coolest thing.

But as an adult, it's one of the things that brings me so many mixed emotions. We met in secret because she wanted to be a part of my life when others didn't.

That's as amazing as it is tragic.

My whole fostering and adoption experience was filled with so many emotional situations at every step.

It was filled with heroes, not villains, but at times filled with pain and heartache. Ultimately, and most importantly, it was filled with love from epic people who cared and who went the extra mile, just for me.

So, in truth, people care, even when you don't feel it.

And it is always a two-way thing. Inside you, right now, is the power to change someone's life for ever. It can be a smile, a handshake, a phone call, an offer of a beer or coffee. That stuff is heroic to some, and we all need that in our lives!

How about right now we write down all the people who care about you?

In the centre of the page, write your own name. Then, around 'you', write the names of all the people in your life who care about you. Write the names of those people who you feel care the most closest to yours. The more you think about it, the more I'm sure you'll find there are quite a few people in your life who care about you a great deal. Sometimes we just don't realise it, but they're there.

Now, think about the last time you checked in on these people. When did you call them, text them or invite them over? Do it now and ask them how they are feeling. Be ready to listen and don't be quick to speak. Once you've done that, listen some more. Hear them like you want to be heard!

CHAPTER 6
FAKE IT TILL YOU
MAKE IT?

While it was difficult to be true to myself when I was in a relationship, it was no easier doing it while single and I often found myself 'faking' parts of my personality and identity, just to get by. Faking that I was OK, faking who I was, faking my personality and beliefs, and faking my confidence.

But the more I faked these things, the more I lost myself, the more I believed I couldn't be the 'real' me, and couldn't live and be accepted in this world.

I felt I had to be 'extra' to be liked and accepted, and that if I faked who I was, if I tried to be like everyone else, I wouldn't be rejected. If I faked it enough, I might actually 'make it' and be accepted!

One of my earliest memories of faking it was when I

started to drink, when I was 16, which led me to developing a fake confidence and persona. Looking back, it coincided with a phase when I felt the deepest hatred towards my face. I wanted to be as far away as possible from my true self. I would copy my friends' personality traits. I would follow their beliefs and thoughts. None of my thoughts or beliefs were original. I observed the environment around me and imitated others as much as I could.

I craved attention. I craved being an 'attractive' human.

In my 16-year-old head I thought: *If my face isn't all that, I'll make my body the best it can be.*

I managed to get a part-time job in the local supermarket, stacking shelfs and working the tills. It was my first experience of work and as much as I hated it, I loved the people who worked there, and they soon began to influence me.

I made a female friend, and she began to take me into the city where we would drink coffee and visit the designer stores.

I remember her telling me that I always needed to have a nice pair of shoes as that is something girls pick up on. After hearing that, I spent all my wages on shoes. I was that easily influenced. Looking back, this person soon became a positive influence in my life. She became a new hero of mine.

As I got older, my relationship with my mum meant I wanted to protect her. It became clear to me that she was a lot older than all the other mums, and, being generations apart, her views on fashion and relationships didn't quite match up with what I wanted. This was also the age when I felt I most needed a dad, one who would have been able to guide me through this period. It was all in my head, a load of bollocks, but that's what I thought back then. This friend took on that role for me and continued to guide me into adulthood.

As I got more comfortable visiting the city, I would travel there alone. Once I had a decent collection of shoes, I began to buy designer clothes. I guess I thought a designer brand would instantly give me cool points, and I *still* needed all the cool points I could get.

My friend helped me find a hairdresser and, before I knew it, I had a stylist and a colour specialist that cost a couple of hundred pounds each time I visited.

I needed these things: they became a part of my identity.

Create the best package, I thought. *You need a reason for someone to like you. You can people-please, you can drop all your boundaries, but you still need something that they'll like about you.*

If a girl did like me, what was she going to say to her friends about me? What were her parents going to think of me? Every parent wants their daughter to bring home Prince Charming, and I felt far from that. *Create something they can take home, create something that they want to share with their parents about you, sell them a reason not to leave you!*

I faked my confidence and faked being this happy person. Continuing to hide my true feelings and emotions, every aspect of my life became fake, even the stories I told were often exaggerated or lies. I needed to impress, but the real me and my true life wouldn't impress anyone.

Nobody wanted to hear my sadness, nobody wanted to know my pain. So I faked being happy and having it all together.

Emotionally and physically, I became so conflicted.

The battle was: *Can I be myself?* Was that even possible, or should I try everything to just fit into this world and what it expects of me? Deep down, I'd have settled for just getting by with a little less pain and conflict.

I soon became obsessed with my body. Not its health, but the way it looked.

I wanted abs 24/7, 365 days a year, so I worked out every day – no rest, just rotating exercises, allowing each body part to rest on the days when I trained others. I trained around injuries, I trained around fatigue, I trained around whatever my schedule was. Training always took priority. I needed to train to make my body perfect. I needed that perfect body for people to like me.

I've always loved food – remember the pizzas? As a kid I would eat everything and anything in sight, but as I got older I really struggled with food. I wasn't bothered about the taste, the experience or the pleasure that comes with food. It became fuel, the minimum amount of fuel that I could get by on.

I limited myself to only eating oats with water for breakfast, and then chicken and vegetables for dinner and tea. My relationship with food became very negative. I tried to massively reduce the fats, sugar and carbs that I ate. I thought they were 'bad' foods and they would prevent me from getting and maintaining my abs, but our bodies *need* good fats and carbs to function. Plus, our bodies look epic when we eat these foods and we fuel ourselves and eat properly. More importantly, they function better too, but I couldn't get my head around that at all. I even limited my water intake: I would sip water because when I drank 'too much', my tummy would look larger. That's normal; it's supposed to happen. But I couldn't process this. All I thought was that I'd lose my abs, and so I would punish myself even more with a harder workout and a stricter diet.

I then became obsessed with sunbeds. I felt I needed a tan as it showed off my muscles more.

I ran in the sauna – actually jogging on the spot – to dehydrate myself, so I looked even more defined, and in social situations I would try and show off my body because I believed that was all that I had to offer.

I knew it was all wrong. In fact, when I was 17 years old, I was studying sports science and so I knew how to fuel my body and that it needed rest. But I still ignored it, all because

I couldn't see certain benefits in the mirror – all in pursuit of being someone I wasn't, trying to be someone that another person would want to be with. But even after all that effort, nobody wanted me. Nobody wanted me and I still had no love for myself. I was going nowhere.

Despite my growing knowledge of diet, wellness and exercise, I ignored it all and followed my hard regime religiously. It became an unhealthy, non-negotiable part of my life and when I wasn't able to maintain it, I really struggled to leave the house or think about anything else. All I could think about was *How can I make up for that?*

I punished myself daily in pursuit of a look I thought I needed in order to be accepted. I would stand in front of the mirror, look at my body and analyse every inch of it. I saw myself as fat and would punish myself with even harder workouts and more extreme diets. The language I used towards myself was becoming meaner and meaner. I still couldn't look at my face, but I would stare and pull at my body and tell myself it wasn't good enough: *I've eaten too much, I've not worked hard enough, I need to spend more time in the sauna.* I was horrible to myself.

Our bodies naturally change throughout the day, throughout the year, throughout our whole lives in fact, and that's totally amazing. But I didn't understand this at all when I had a fake mindset hiding my true emotions, thoughts and feelings.

I had a fake, fragile confidence, and if any part of my routine didn't happen, I felt defeated: what had I missed, what had I done wrong? I kept going back to the routine to try and get it back on track.

I've always played out situations in my head. I would run through scenarios and have conversations with the people in those scenarios. There was one involving another girl asking the girl who was seeing me, 'Why are you dating Jono? What do you see in him?'

The girl that was seeing me would reply, 'Well, I know his face isn't all that, but his body is hot, and he'll do anything for me.'

So in my head, they now had a reason to date me.

My entire identity became focused on my need for another person – to be complete, to be whole, to be happy – and I faked it all in the hope I could achieve this.

My daily routine soon took over my life. It went as follows:

My day started with porridge oats and water, then I would train.

After training, five minutes of jogging on the spot in the sauna before a shower.

Sunbed and then home with a protein shake (again, made with water).

Once home, I would shave everywhere.

I would trim my hair if it needed it and then straighten it.

Next, put some expensive aftershave on.

Then to clothes. (I would wear tops or jackets just once so that I wouldn't be seen in them again).

Accessorise with watches, chains and rings.

Trainers. (I had a big collection by then.)

Perhaps choose another shit tattoo upon a whim.

All this just to leave the house.

All this just to get by.

Lunch – one chicken breast and a pack of frozen veg.

Tea – same again.

Fake tan before bed.

Repeat.

Throughout the whole day, I'd look at my stomach and pull the bits of skin that I could grab, hurling abuse at myself if I got any of it wrong.

I was walking around with a fake smile and this fake attitude, and to look at me, I think people would have assumed I was doing OK. But in truth I was a dehydrated, underweight mess, complete with a shit crucifix tattoo on my arm!

I never really knew how exhausting it was until I grew

out of the need for doing it. This wasn't specifically something that I worked on, but something that slowly disappeared when I accidentally found things that I liked about myself – more on that later!

But the less I faked things, the more energy I had!

I've recognised that a lot of new relationships and connections that I made during this period weren't based on truth, which made it hard to create safe foundations with people. Some relationships were completely fake too. People weren't getting to know the real me. That was on me, not them. I prevented them from getting to know the real me and, instead, gave them a version of me that I thought they wanted. It stunted my growth and prevented so many natural opportunities. Although I thought my life was getting easier and more fulfilling, it was actually getting further away from where I wanted to be.

When it comes to health care, food, exercise and the words that we use to motivate ourselves, these things should always come from a place of love and be constructive. There needs to be a balance. They should always add to your life, and none of them should become a dependency.

If you've done something you're not proud of, it's OK to be critical and admit your wrongs, but don't be too hard on yourself.

If you want that cake, eat that cake. If you want another slice, go for it. Just know that you need to nurture your body with movement, prayer and good foods too.

Thankfully, I now love a lot about myself: I love that I'm very true to all my feelings and actions.

I share my true thoughts and feelings, whatever they may be.

I train when I want, and I enjoy it. Sometimes I throw weights about. Sometimes they are heavy and other times they are light.

Sometimes I run, hike or climb.

I'll attend a yoga class or do some guided meditation.

I rest when I need to and don't punish myself for allowing myself that rest. That rest can be a day on the sofa, or a week of just being chilled out.

I've not seen a sunbed or used fake tan in years. Now I have to moisturise my skin to keep it softer.

I will enjoy a beer or a glass of wine.

I will eat all the pizza that I can get my hands on, followed by a dessert.

I'll try to be healthier before a holiday, ready to wear

my short shorts in the sun. And I'll overindulge on those holidays.

With less obsession over my appearance, I now have more time for lie-ins and naps, but the best bit is that my life, my world, feels better for it. My body is my home, my safe place, and it might come in all kinds of forms but that's totally fucking epic. I definitely don't need another person in order to feel whole.

I now have this saying, 'kale and ale'. While physical healing or healthy mental wellness is a balance, it's not always *balanced*. You may go through phases where self-medicating is your medicine. Having a strong partner, friend, spiritual practice or therapist can help you decide when you're overindulging or self-medicating too much. But the 'kale and ale' principle – the idea of balancing healthy habits with less healthy ones – means that sometimes you're on the kale but sometimes you're on the ale.

You can't have the perfect ratio every day. But what brings you back into balance is the fact that you know you need both. You know you can have both, and you know that sometimes you'll be more one than the other. You can also self-heal too much and create an unhealthy image of being healthy (for instance, with orthorexia, when you obsess too much about eating 'pure' foods but end up malnourished).

Are you currently faking anything, or are you turning up as your true authentic self?

What's your relationship with food and exercise like?

When was the last time the way your body looked actually made you a friend or got you a job? Probably never, right?!

What do you say to yourself when you look in the mirror? Are you kind to yourself, or do you beat yourself up and punish yourself?

The language and thoughts that we aim towards ourselves every day are life-changing ones.

For example, as I have shared, all my thoughts and the language that I used to use about my face were negative and they consumed me. Most of us have done this. But if we flip these negatives to positive thoughts, the positive ones can consume us too.

When I spoke about myself or shared my story I would say things like, 'My birth parents left me because of my face.' It reinforced the pain and hate that I felt inside.

Now I say, 'Me and my parents went our separate ways.' This reinforces a more healing, calmer mindset.

Here's another example. When I would struggle to do a task, like lifting a heavy weight in the gym, I'd think of a time that I got bullied and, as I visualised it, I'd say to myself, 'Jono, quit being weak and prove all the bullies wrong.'

Anger would help me lift, for sure, but that lift, that motivation, came from an unhealthy place, again making me relive the pain over and over again.

Now I say, 'Come on, Jonny Boy, you got this,' and I lift.

The same outcome but motivated by a healthier fuel – you gotta get with the times and get a more sustainable, healthier fuel!

I accidentally discovered that people kind of dig your authentic self more than a fake version of you. When you experience this for yourself, it means you've opened yourself up to allow life-changing connections to happen.

At 19 I had experienced those challenging relationships, worked out a stupid amount, was regularly speaking to myself with the most hateful of words and I wasn't sharing any of my feelings or dark thoughts.

My friends were going on holidays and going to university. Some of them were even having kids and getting married. I began to hide away, believing none of this would happen for me. But despite me hiding and pushing everyone away, my friends still invited me to every event and included me in everything. I still said no, but I was always invited.

One of my best friends saw that I was struggling and one day, as we were talking, he could see I needed some life energy injected into me.

He asked me how I was doing, how work was going, and I just told him it was shit. I didn't go into it any further, other than saying everything was shit.

So he goes, 'Mate, why don't you come and work with me at this bar? The chicks are hot and we just drink while we work. It's the best job ever, you'll love it.'

With my experience of bars and girls, I thought: *No, I don't think so, it sounds like hell.*

But after several conversations, debates and arguments with him, I gave in and decided to give it a try.

My friend lent me a work T-shirt and told me I could start on Thursday. Once he had gone, I was back alone with my thoughts. *What am I doing? Why me? Why does everything have to be so hard?* But the lad inside me was saying: *I might just enjoy this!*

The conflict in my head was torture – the fear mixed with a craving to live and love life.

This craving to live and love life was buried deep within me, buried below the basic need to survive. So on this occasion, I was proud that I had taken a leap of faith and gone for something that I really wanted to do.

My friend told me that the uniform was trousers of my choice and the work T-shirt that said 'Frankie says reflex' – a twist on the epic 1980s anthem.

That week I hammered the gym, training every muscle group. I watched everything I ate, and upped my minutes on the sunbed. *I need to look my best to get through this*, I thought.

My first shift came around. I was nervous and excited. Being excited about something was rare for me.

That day, I followed my daily routine and wore my uniform, which I had customised. (I had to put 'me' into the outfit.) It's weird, but I often found that, with clothing, I enjoyed wearing things that made me stand out. Even at the parties we had in high school, I had to stand out. Maybe I was trying to take away the focus from my face again, I don't know. I was even driving around in a bright green car and owned a Backstreet Boys T-shirt. If you went through my wardrobe there were a lot of standout pieces, to be honest.

So back to this work T-shirt: how could I stand out from all the others in this? I grabbed the kitchen scissors that I used to do my hair with and cut the shirt into what I thought was a better fit. To me, that was making it shorter so that when I reached up you would see some skin peeping out from the bottom of my T-shirt. Then I cut slits all over the top, to show more of my fake-baked, suntanned skin (yes, sad, I know).

That day, I spent 12 minutes under the fake rays of the sunbed, and my hair was straightened. (I was going through an emo phase and had a black streak running through my blond hair too.) I had my customised uniform on, with my chest and arms on show, and I'd smashed the gym.

I started my first shift as the best fake, fragile-confident version of myself I could have created. The student nights were the busiest, and my friend gave me the heads-up that you met so many new people and the potential to pull was huge. This made me even more nervous. I hated meeting new people who hadn't seen my face before. I was a nervous wreck, to say the least. I don't even remember getting to the bar that night. My first memory of that night is of standing behind the bar on my own, thinking, *What the hell am I doing here?*

As I was stood behind the bar with those thoughts going through my head, I turned to my left and saw my friend laughing and joking with all the other staff. A small thought crept into my head: *I wish I was him right now.* (I had so many moments in my life when I thought this: *Anyone but me.*)

The DJ was working his way through the 1980s anthems, the fridges were full of alcopops and I'd familiarised myself with the surroundings and the way the till worked.

My friend came over and did a quick check-in with me. He had a massive smile on his face and was dancing along to the music as he went around the bar. My heart was racing, literally about to burst out of my chest.

At 7pm the doors were unlocked, and we were open for business. My heart was beating faster and faster with the anticipation of a huge crowd walking through the doors, but nobody did. Not a soul entered the bar. Nobody came in for the first half an hour and my heart settled a little. A few people started coming in for drinks. The experienced staff quickly served them and they made their way to the dance floor to showcase their dodgy dance moves.

I was in no rush to serve anyone. I was happier getting boxes of bottles from the cellar. But by 9pm the bar was beginning to get busy. The students were ready for an epic night; they'd been studying all day and were craving alco-pops to help them forget all their troubles.

The first few people I served were easy. I didn't make eye contact, quickly grabbed and served their drinks, received their money and moved on to the next person. Job done.

I watched them all interact with one another and kind of felt like I was there, but not really a part of any of it.

I wasn't engaging in conversation. There were no jokes, no smiles: *Just serve them so they can move on from me.*

As the night wore on, the bar became busier and busier and soon every dark thought was entering my head: *I don't belong here.* All I could hear were the voices, the comments. All I could see were stares, pointing and laughing. I don't know if it was all in my head, but at the time I felt all the negative feelings that I had experienced in life as if they were happening right now behind that bar. I wanted to disappear. *I don't belong here!*

I needed to escape. I was only a couple of hours into my first shift, but I needed to go. I didn't say anything to anyone, but I grabbed my things, got my head down and walked through the back door to the nearest taxi rank. This was an all too familiar experience, leaving early, leaving alone, wanting to find a place where I belonged, where I felt wanted.

When I arrived home, who was there at the door waiting for me? My Mama Jean, full of love and full of intrigue.

'How's it gone?' she asked.

She showed up as she always did, ready to listen, ready to console, in whatever way I needed.

This person would, and still will, do absolutely anything to keep me safe, to give me comfort.

I wanted to share how much I was hurting and how lost I was. I really did. I wanted to open up more than anything.

But all I could do was put on my biggest fake smile and just casually say, 'I'm OK, it just wasn't for me. The money, the hours, not for me.'

She smiled and gave me the biggest hug. Looking back, deep down I think she knew I was hurting, maybe not how deeply I was hurting, but she knew. And I kept it all from her, thinking that I was somehow protecting her. One of my biggest support links was broken because I refused to open up.

I went up to my room again, hating my face, hating my life. *If I can't do it with all this effort, how can I ever do it by just being me?*

That weekend, I didn't do anything. I barely ate or drank. I just slept. I didn't even have the desire to phone the randoms whose attention I once craved. There was nothing left in me. I was empty. I just existed.

The weekend passed. The next week, my friend came back to me.

'There's hotter girls, mate, more epic nights to be had. You've got to come back, dude.'

I didn't tell him what had happened at my first shift. Had he even noticed that I'd left? I don't know, but he was there for a reason. He'd recognised the need to stand in front of me, getting me to step out into the world again.

I can't express enough that I had no desire to go back to the bar, but somehow my friend, with a fresh uniform, managed to persuade me to head back.

The following week, student night again, the routine was complete: the uniform was on and I stood behind the bar, alone, nervous, feeling sick, with my friend nearby having the time of his life. I wished I was him. I tried my best, but even faking it I couldn't access any of that.

Like clockwork, at 7pm the doors opened. Once again, serving the first few people was easy.

But again, the busier it became, the louder it became. The only thing I could feel was all the negativity that lived in my head.

I felt the need to leave again, but before I could a guy walked into the bar and as he walked in I accidentally made eye contact with him. He was huge, covered head to toe in tattoos and had muscles on his muscles that I didn't even know existed.

He made a beeline straight to my side of the bar. When he got there, he took out his money and just leaned over the bar and stared at me.

I knew he was going to say something to me, so I looked away and prayed that someone else would serve him before I could get to him.

I just knew he was going to make my night a living nightmare.

I was serving people, from right to left at the bar, and my heart was racing faster and faster the closer I got to him.

I need to get out of here.

Obviously, nobody else served the guy and I suddenly found my myself standing in front of him, looking at my own feet.

I asked him what he would like to drink.

With no hesitation, he eagerly replies, 'Hold up, mate.

Before you get me my drink, what happened to your face? Why do you look like that?'

I cringed. I wanted the ground to swallow me up whole. I hated talking about my face, especially in public. Again I asked, 'What would you like to drink?'

He still hadn't got the message. He still hadn't read that I was incredibly uncomfortable. 'What's happened to your ears, why are they like that?'

I mumbled that I was born like this. 'What would you like to drink?'

Again, he's not quite ready for that drink yet and points to my hearing aid. 'That's a hearing aid. What can you hear without your hearing aid?'

'Nothing, mate,' I said.

He then smiled. 'You can't hear anything? Nothing at all? Mate, you're so lucky. I wish I had that option, to pick and choose when I can and can't hear.'

'Why?' I asked.

'Well, mate, I've got a wife at home and she's so loud. She doesn't stop. As soon as I get home it's like someone has just charged her mouth up and she doesn't stop talking. She doesn't even pause for air. I'd do anything for some peace at times.'

I laughed, looked up at him with a smile and shared that when I'm fed up with people or life in general, I just turn my hearing aid off. I love that I can do that.

Then something amazing happened.

He asked me what my name was.

As I told him my name, he held out his hand, gave me his name and we shared a handshake.

He said, 'Nice to meet you,' and asked me what I was drinking.

I got us both a drink, we cheersed and then off he went into the night.

Now this moment might not seem significant to you, but that moment, that offer of a handshake, changed my life for ever.

See? I got him all wrong. I was living in my negative head and I assumed he was going to be mean towards me, that he had an agenda to hurt me like others had done in the past, to make a joke at my expense for his own and others' entertainment.

But the truth is, he just wanted to know, he wanted to connect. Yes, his approach or language could have been more discreet, but I recognise that some people don't have the background or words to do it any other way than the ways they know and they may, at times, be a little forward or abrupt.

As he left me that night, my eyes had opened. I looked around and realised that I didn't know what people were speaking about. I didn't know what they were laughing at, but it was more likely people were laughing with their friends about their own lives rather than at me.

I'd like to think I'm the centre of the universe (we all do sometimes), but the truth is I'm not. Life is happening all around me, and people usually focus more on their own stuff than on me.

There will always be moments when people are unkind, but getting rid of my assumption that everyone is like that was a game-changer for me.

After that encounter, I didn't go home as early that night. I worked with my head held a little higher and I went out with my friends afterwards.

I wouldn't say it was a lightbulb moment, more that someone turned the brightness up ever so slightly.

I continued to work in the bar, still heavily relying on my routine, but now I had more of a social life and more of an understanding of the bar job being the 'best job ever': 'the chicks are hot, we drink while we work' kind of thing.

Weeks went by and then a new girl started working in the bar. She wore a beret, military jacket, skinny jeans and a necklace with a giant plastic red heart on it. She loved Morrissey and the Smiths, did ballet and always loved to dance.

I couldn't help but admire the way she moved through life. I thought she was the coolest person I'd ever laid eyes on.

When we spoke, I felt a pull towards her. I wanted to know everything about her, but I held myself back. I thought, *Why would she, a super-cool chick, be interested in a guy like me?*

The days at the bar flew by. I wouldn't say I had stopped faking it just yet. In fact, as I was around this girl I invested in my routine a little more: maybe I could create something that would catch her eye. I still needed to fake my smile, I still hid all my fears from those around me, but I was living a little more. That was something and I'd take that right now.

One night at the bar, the cool beret-wearing girl danced through the crowd towards me and casually asked me if I wanted to grab a drink with her at some point. I didn't think anything of it. My natural response was, 'Yes, we're all going out after work, you should join us!'

She smiled, and replied, 'No, I mean just you and me.'

This had never happened to me before – girls didn't ask me out for a drink – so I was in new territory here. I wanted to play it cool, but I had the biggest, cheesiest grin on my face and a bad case of verbal diarrhoea.

'Yeah, I'm free Monday, Tuesday, Wednesday, Thursday, Friday, Saturday and Sunday. When do you want to make this happen?'

She was way cooler and more chilled out than me and said, 'I can do tomorrow evening if you want to hang out.'

Obviously that worked for me.

We arranged a time and a place. I suggested a cinema date – poor choice of date but I had very little experience in date planning – and she led the way with the rest, suggesting the day and time and asking if I could pick her up. 'Yes, yes and yes.' Anything to make this happen as it might never happen again.

I gave an awkward 'See you then' and we went our separate ways back to our homes that night.

Mum was no longer waiting by the door these days, but she always heard me come in and would shout, 'Hey, love!' as I walked up to my room.

'Night,' I'd shout and get ready for bed.

That night I couldn't sleep, though. Every thought was going through my head.

I could never just enjoy a moment. I had to work out what the motive was, what was her agenda?

I was thinking: *Why? Why does she want to see me? Will she turn up? Will she cancel? Why ask me out?*

It might not even be a date, so don't overthink it.

She might only want to get to know me so she can ask one of my friends out.

I was giving myself this pep talk: *Don't build it up to something massive 'cos you'll just end up disappointed, people just see you as a nice guy, nothing more.*

The morning came and I started my routine: gym,

sauna, sunbed, new clothes. Feeling the pressure to look my best, I gave myself an extra hour to get ready . . .

I've always talked to myself, so I was now giving myself the biggest pep talk ever at this point, trying to build myself up in every way possible while also preparing myself for rejection and disappointment.

By this time, I had learned to drive and managed to save up the wages from my supermarket job to buy a little boy-racer Renault Clio. Instead of buying trainers, it was wheels, window tints and chrome exhausts. *The girls will love this.*

On our first date at the cinema, we saw the worst movie ever and afterwards I literally dropped her off back home, sat in the car motionless and said goodnight (cinema dates don't work, guys). But somehow after that first date I managed to get a second and a third, and I want to share one date that has stayed with me, when we went for a walk around a local dam.

Even though we had been on several dates, I still had the same feelings – *Will she turn up? Why does she want to spend time with me? This is too good to be true. All good things end eventually.* Even today I can feel like this when good things are happening. Somewhere deep down there's a learned behaviour that good things don't happen to me – and if they do, they don't last (it's something that I'm working on).

So, the day of the dam, we're a few dates in, I hammered

my routine and I arrived early in my Clio. I was nervous and sweaty. However, I was prepared, so I put on a fresh shirt once I got there and I waited in my car. *Will she even turn up?*

The minutes passed and they felt like hours. I was looking around in every direction. She wasn't even late, but I was convinced she wasn't coming.

She arrived on time, wearing her skinny jeans and military jacket. I got out of my car with a big sigh of relief: *She's here, that's a start.*

She walked towards me. Even her walk was cool. She gave me a hug and just started talking to me. She was just so cool and it all looked so easy. I felt shy and awkward at first, just trying to focus on what she was saying, but I was still wondering about all the 'whys'. It seemed I could never be in the moment because my mind wandered to those dark places.

But her energy allowed me to relax, and eventually I felt myself in the moment.

I started to share, I laughed, I opened up, for the first time in my life. We accidentally made contact and I felt sparks. Her arm brushed mine as we walked side by side and I liked it. I wanted more of that closeness.

To my amazement, she was listening and sharing right back, literally about everything and anything, not just surface-level stuff but deep stuff too, stuff that people don't usually talk about.

It was getting colder and darker, and we were getting to the end of the designated path. I was walking more slowly because I really didn't want it to end.

And then again in her cool, effortless way she was like, 'Are you coming back to mine?'

In my uncool, desperate way, I said, 'Yeah, definitely,' with my big cheesy grin.

We got into my car and she dived straight into my CD collection (remember those?), playing DJ while also criticising all the rap CDs I had in there.

She put on some music she could sing along to before I set off. Needless to say, we didn't listen to any rap on the way to hers.

Before we got there, we picked up some vegetarian microwavable curries and a cheap bottle of red wine.

Next stop: her place.

I say her place – it was shared cheap student accommodation, and after briefly meeting her housemates we went to the kitchen.

I was nervous. I didn't know where this was going but I knew there was no other place I'd rather be.

The meals were zapped in the microwave, the wine was opened, and she took me upstairs to her room. She lit some candles and put on some Jeff Buckley.

Once the mood was set, we sat on the bedroom floor ready to tuck into the (for me) best meal ever. The conversation was still flowing and I was still feeling those sparks of energy, that feeling of ease and the comfort of being myself.

Once we had eaten our food, we finished the bottle of wine together. Then, for the first time that day, she became lost for words, and the words she did choose were carefully picked from her vast, university-influenced vocabulary. I knew what was coming. I knew what that meant. It always happened when people tried to find the right words to start the conversation about my face. There was no malice in it, but they were being careful not to offend me.

I accepted it from strangers. I didn't mind it from people I knew, but in this situation, with a girl that I fancied, I thought: *My face isn't sexy, this isn't a cool conversation*, and I didn't want to be having it.

So, as we were sat face to face on the floor, and she was being careful with her words, I was looking at the same floor, feeling disappointed. The girl that I had been looking at all evening, I could no longer look at. I was embarrassed.

She said, 'Jono, I find myself staring at you all the time.'

With those words, I thought: *I hate being stared at. This isn't a date, I've got this wrong.*

She was trying to make eye contact with me and before I had a chance to say anything else she said, 'I just love your face,' and leaned in and kissed me.

I was kissing the girl I fancied the most, like, ever.

With that single kiss, I went from feeling unattractive to thinking I was the sexiest guy in the world.

I was my own friggin' superhero right then.

I could have easily cancelled our date. I could have so easily turned down that job or never gone back to the bar, but for once I had done what all heroes do: I turned up when things got tough. At some point that day, I stopped faking it and I was being myself, and this cool chick absolutely loved it.

For the first time in ages, I turned up as Jono, with no bullshit, and not only did she vibe off of that, so did I!

This was absolutely huge for me, and for the first time I got a sense of the people I attracted when I was being my authentic self!

This was another game-changer for me.

The connection on a deeper level, the sparks, the sharing of truths, the eye contact, my quirks, my individuality all worked on this day and I started to believe it could work on any given day.

I hadn't discovered self-love yet – but I was on my way, and it started with another person recognising things they loved about me first. Ultimately, those were things I could love about myself. We were on to something here. I just needed time, I just needed to keep on being my own hero and turning up as Jono when things got scary.

As I look back at my life, I've made the best connections when I've been my unfiltered, authentic self, and this is how you will make the most long-lasting and meaningful connections in your life too.

What do you currently do to help yourself manage social interactions? I'm sure that you have some really useful tricks and habits, alongside some potentially unhelpful ones too.

Do you drink before you go out? Do you spend money that you haven't got on clothes and products? Do you train when your body is crying for rest? Do you act up or play a part that has come to be expected of you?

You know I did.

I want you to write down the things that you currently do to manage social interactions.

Now, write down what you want to get out of the social interactions/events that you go to.

Ask yourself this: will drinking, or dressing a certain way (whatever you wrote), help you achieve this?

Asking yourself these questions will help you get in touch with what you want out of the experience and decide if your current habits are actually helpful.

For me now, going out is about dressing in my quirky style (sometimes new stuff, sometimes old, some charity shop finds and the odd luxury item I can afford). I do like to drink but I'm aware of my limit. I won't beat myself up if I haven't trained and I'll always have a graceful, respectful exit plan prepared in advance, so I don't give away all my time or overstay my welcome.

Throughout my life, I had battled with thoughts about an absent father.

But as I was becoming more full of self-love, I recognised that I had a lot of father figures in my life: my adoptive brother would always take me to rugby and football games; my adoptive sister was one of the first people to do movie nights with me and to drink with me; there was also a PE teacher in the final year of high school who I became close with. Even watching my friends become fathers helped me see that I was surrounded by them, but by obsessing over the one that wasn't there, I don't think I appreciated what I already had.

I have learned, though, that I can be a man but not necessarily 'masculine' (a word I don't really use).

I love and celebrate the fact that I was raised by a single mother, one who was a couple of generations older than me too.

Through her, from the earliest of stages, I was raised to

talk about my feelings. I was able to say when I was scared, and if I cried my mum would cry with me. Yes, I lost these skills along the way, but they've always been a part of me.

As I've grown older I have noticed that I'm very different from my male friends. In the past I've been told I 'look gay' or that I 'act gay'. The more I've found myself, the more I've celebrated who I am. The more authentic I've found myself being, the more confidence I've had to act how I truly feel. I've begun to talk more openly about my emotions and openly cry, and while all of this is not 'typical' male behaviour, I didn't tend to notice. It only really became apparent to me when I started to go on stag dos with my friends.

My friends have invited me to every single one of their stag dos, and all their dads go too, so they always invite my mum. She's turned down every one but it's so ace that she's been invited.

But when I interact and spend time with the dads, I genuinely don't know how to act or what to do. My friends have been brought up with a father who they have hung out with, and gone to the pub with, which I think builds a social code and practice that is so alien to me.

On these stag dos, everyone's full of banter and I'm just awkward, occasionally overstepping the mark with an unintentional insult, talking about emotions at the wrong time. While all the lads are having pints, I'm requesting sangria, and while the lads are talking football I'm talking about my latest yoga class and my love for Lululemon leggings (they're incredible by the way!).

I'm not sure if any of this is making any sense, but in a world where the rate of male suicide is high and continues to increase, I feel incredibly lucky that I was raised the way I was by a woman who allowed me to be soft and vulnerable – and that's a strength that's going to keep me safe for the rest of my life.

So I will continue to cry and continue to open up, and I will continue to encourage everyone around me to do the same.

Being brave and showing who you are to others will only strengthen your feelings of self-love. There is a pressure from society to behave in certain ways. It can be challenging to go against these expectations and be your authentic self, but the rewards for doing so can be huge.

As I've shared my work online and my platform has grown across social media, I've been invited to speak at events, where more people see and experience how I am and then ask me to do more events. My therapist tells me I'm a healer.

I've been lucky enough to travel and I've had the opportunity to meet many others that had a pain inside them that they were keeping a secret.

After I speak I always stay behind at the event, and if I've spoken at a school or university, I will actually spend the day there as I know people will come up to me wanting to share or ask questions in a more private setting.

I've noticed a lot of common trends in these moments. The youngest kids, the four- to ten-year-olds, will share pretty much everything with me – things that they haven't even shared with their guardians or parents. I always have a teacher or a counsellor nearby when I do this so we can seek support for a student if needed.

Between 10 and 16 years old, though, kids become more reluctant to share things. At this stage in their lives, they have very adult thoughts but don't have the life skills to process them. It's at this age that they start to send me letters and emails, sharing their thoughts more privately.

I can typically split adults into two categories. It may sound like a generalisation, but women will usually come up to me and share it all; they will give me a hug and cry, they will thank me, then message me again later with more thoughts and more appreciation. But with the men it's a completely different story.

Most men will wait behind, even if it means being the last one in the queue, and when it comes to their turn they will hold out their hand and give me a handshake and say thank you.

The more I've become aware of this difference, the more I've done a little digging in these moments. I'll ask the men:

'How did you find that?'

'Did anything affect you?'

'Have you felt any of those things that I've spoken about?'

More often than not they then slowly start to open up. Some still keep quiet, but some will eventually send me a message and express their feelings.

Once, at a three-day event I was speaking at, we set up a men-only group discussion, and someone in this group echoed feelings that I'd had in my early twenties, things which many of us have felt in our lives.

Before I share what he said, I should explain that there is a code in these groups that whatever is said stays within the group, but this gentlemen has kindly allowed me to share his story, as we believe that sharing thoughts and feelings out loud is a powerful healing experience. For some this can be easier to do within the same peer group, particularly when it comes to men.

So, during the three days, we held these group discussions and we shared everything, from pain to fears. We shared, we listened, and we gave one another advice and comforting words.

On the final day one gentleman still hadn't spoken, so

we gave him some encouragement and asked if he wanted to share anything with the group.

He leaned forward and with a softly spoken voice began to share.

'I'm well educated, I have real estate, I like fine wine, I'm on the board of a non-profit and love nice clothes, but I see myself as a failure as I have never even kissed a woman.'

There was silence. For a moment, no one spoke. We just sat with the information and we felt it; we were connected.

I felt that we'd all been there at some point in our lives.

He thanked us for listening and continued to tell us that it was the first time he had shared this information with anyone, and that it felt good.

Everyone began to talk and console each other. It brought everyone closer. I felt this power.

What people or environments in your life make you feel like your most authentic self?

When do you feel that you can drop your guard down and share some real thoughts?

What is it about these people and places that allow you to feel safe and at ease?

When do you find yourself having to wear an emotional mask or put on the fake smile?

NOT ALL HEROES WEAR CAPES

Who are you with?

By being aware of your environment (people and places) on a daily basis, you can feel reassured that you have safe places and people that help you to be more open and relaxed, to fill your own cup up.

This will help you get through the more professional environments and enable you to manage your day or week based on what energy you need.

For instance, a busy working week in the office Monday to Thursday (energy drainer) means I need a slow healing yoga class or some beers with the gang on Friday (energy filler).

CHAPTER 7
THERE'S A SUPERHERO
INSIDE OF YOU

Have you ever bought a new outfit for a Christmas party or some event that you were attending, and when you tried it on it gave you an instant lift, an instant confidence boost?

Well, in my early twenties I had spent so much of my life searching for those instant lifts to boost my confidence, and if I had continued trying to find them, they would eventually have run out. Or I would have started looking in more dangerous, unhealthy places. As this went on I'd be missing out on opportunities to do the real work on my trauma and focus on my needs.

It was now time to address these things and do something for myself.

By the time I was 21, via my mum, my friend at the bar,

and my secret grandma, that crazy daily routine and a lot of dodgy haircuts, I had reached a point where I was OK. I was happy.

Then the girl I met in the bar ended things because she wanted to travel, which kind of made me like her even more. This badass girl was just out to live her life, and nothing was going to stop her.

This kind of rubbed off on me and I thought: *What do I want to do beyond working in a bar?*

What were my goals? What did I want in life? I had to revisit these as I had given up on so many goals and dreams in the past, I had to do the work and find them again.

> When was the last time you revisited your goals or your bucket list?
>
> Let's write them down. What are your goals for the next 12 months? If you have goals beyond that, great, write them down too, but if not don't worry because living in the now is hugely important and that's where I am currently. Living in the now.
>
> But what I *really* want to know is . . .
>
> What's on your bucket list too? However far-fetched things may seem, let's get them written down.

In my early twenties I was still discovering my passions, dreams and goals, and I still had a massive passion for fitness. I thought about working in a gym, but despite having a little more confidence I thought: *How can I work in an industry where people obsess over their image? How can I work in a place that has mirrors on every wall? Surely it's a place for perfect tanned bodies and surely it's a place where I don't belong?*

But the dream was there, so I wrote down what I needed to do to get there.

Even though I hadn't gone to university, I still needed some qualifications, so that was the first step: a two-week intensive course to become a fitness instructor.

I smashed it. I liked this new confidence and direction I had. It made sense, it took pressure off me and made life seem simpler.

We didn't have job search companies back then, so it was a case of printing your CV out and handing it in to the places where you wanted a job.

On my days off from the bar, I grabbed a pile of my CVs, jumped into my lowered boy-racer Clio (now fitted with a massive boombox that filled 90 per cent of the boot) and dropped my CV off at a few gyms, by literally walking into reception and throwing my CV at the receptionist while looking at the floor.

A few days passed and I received a phone call inviting me for an interview at one of the big gyms in the city.

Without hesitation, I was all in. I think in the past I

would have bottled it. But with my new-found confidence I was able to do some things that scared me.

The day of the interview, I was suited and booted – yes, with freshly trimmed hair – and I arrived an hour early and sat in my car, saying 'Oh, fuck!' repeatedly.

We all have those moments of fear, those moments of *Am I good enough? Can I do this?* going through our heads. We often look back through our life experiences for hope and belief in ourselves. Inside me at that moment, there was an internal war between my heroes and the haters and bullies.

Every interaction that we have with another human being can be used in the future. An interaction may generate a belief that you can 'do it' or it may generate a fear that makes you think you 'can't'. That power is inside you right now.

Thankfully the heroes won that day in the car park, and with hope, belief and the biggest 'Do it!', I got out of my car and headed into the gym.

The receptionist had already learned my name and asked me to sit down and wait for the fitness manager to arrive.

I was so nervous, and I didn't know where to look. Moments later, a ball of energy walked into the gym: the fitness manager, a 6-foot, 5-inch ex-rugby player who now taught aerobics.

The receptionist ran over, jumped on him and gave him the biggest hug. She then introduced me to him, he shook my hand and told me to follow him. I was expecting to go to an office or somewhere private, but he took me to the gym floor and asked me to give him a bit of a workout using various equipment and machinery. So I did.

I have nothing bad to say about this whole experience. We trained a little and he got to know me. We laughed, we joked, and it felt like I had made an instant friend. His energy was beautiful, and I forgot every fear that I had felt in the car park.

The interview ended and I went home. Within an hour, I received a phone call saying that I had got the job and I was buzzing.

Looking back, I think this began one of the happier, more carefree periods of my life.

Having constant access to a gym, sauna and sunbeds meant I became more obsessed with them. I was going out more and still had hopes of dating, so the routine to look my best was still there.

But I was coping with it all. I had a routine and I felt safe and OK with life.

For a while I worked in the gym alongside picking up shifts at the bar, and would combine the bar work with going out with my friends.

I still relied on alcohol to get through the nights out. I watched and listened to my friends brag about all the girls they had slept with and I got jealous when those things didn't happen for me.

Every year, between the ages of 16 and 20, I had refused to join the lads' holiday when they asked. I was full of fear: *I won't pull. I can't do my routine. What would I do with my hearing aid? I would ruin their holiday if we got into a fight because someone had been unkind to me.* No, it wasn't for me.

But that year, at the age of 21, I jumped at the chance to go and off we went to Malia, Greece.

It's mad but going on my first lads' holiday was, at that point, one of the hardest, scariest things I had agreed to do. It was like the parties from my teenage years, but a million times more anxiety-inducing.

I read articles on how to pull and what the latest fashion trends were, and I asked my friends what happened on lads' holidays. I needed to be prepared.

On the day we were set to go, I was so nervous as we all met up at a friend's house. The dads were there telling stories of their own lads' holidays, and with every story my nerves grew.

The minibus arrived and we headed to the airport, while having a few drinks. The rest is a bit of a blur for me. I couldn't believe I was actually doing it.

When we arrived in Malia, there was a foam party on the first day. It was a blessing in disguise, as all the lads wanted to go but I declined and I was honest about why too: I would have to take my hearing aid off and I wouldn't be able to hear anything. I'm not confident without my hearing aid. They were so chill and cool about it. Off they went and it gave me a moment to compose myself. I did a home workout (obvs!) and began to get ready for the night.

Once they were back, we continued to drink, we listened to Biggie and played drinking games before heading out on to the strip.

The strip was tough for me. All my friends were chatting to girls and even had a competition running for who could sleep with the most people. I didn't take part.

On the first night I met two girls who worked in a bar at one end of the strip, so most nights I would be with the lads and, once they pulled, I would head back to this bar and hang out with these girls. They became friends. I was good at making those. Although I was scared of girls romantically, I've always been comfortable being friends with them.

The best thing about this holiday was that Greece, who didn't have the best national football team by a long shot, won the 2004 Euros, beating Portugal. It's one of the biggest football upsets of recent times. The whole island celebrated. I remember there being tractors, diggers and cars driving down the street with people hanging off them, with flares, horns and microphones. Fireworks lit up the night sky. It was insane. One of my favourite things about this trip was that it meant I finally had a memory with the boys that I was in on: a story that we can talk about down the years and I can say I was there. I was one of the boys.

As I said, life was good. Dating sucked, but I came to realise it sucks for everyone, especially at that age. Even so, finding another person was still the biggest thing for me and I felt incomplete if I wasn't experiencing that.

I had experienced different partners and intimacy, and I wanted more of it.

I would get desperately drunk on nights out in the hope of experiencing it. But the truth is, I was looking for love in the wrong kinds of places and I was actually looking for the wrong type of love too.

Life-changing moments happen at the most unexpected times and during this period I had one of those moments. It happened purely by accident too: it wasn't planned, it wasn't due to work that I had done intentionally, but nonetheless I experienced the biggest energy shift at the gym.

I'd done the bar job, I'd gone out with my friends, they

had all hooked up with someone or were in a relationship already, and I thought I had failed. Even when things were going well, I still had these daily doubts and setbacks, sometimes for brief moments and sometimes for a day or two, but thankfully they eventually passed.

It was a slow day at the gym and I always worked the late shift, 3pm till 10pm.

By 9.30pm the gym was empty. At this time, it was often just me, the receptionist and, maybe, a cleaner.

There's this phenomenon that happens in almost every gym: people can take the weights off the rack, they can lift them, often doing up to 30 reps between breaks, but once they have finished it's nearly impossible for them to put them back, which means the sparrow-legged new fitness instructor (me) had to put them all away at 9.30pm before we locked up.

I was putting all the weights away and, in every gym, the free weights are always in front of the world's biggest mirrors (still the things I hated the most).

I was putting the weights away and trying to avoid seeing my face in the mirror. I had just bought some new trainers, so I was admiring my new kicks. I had my short shorts on, so I started to check out my legs and butt and thought I had a cute butt.

I was on a roll. I had just trained my upper body and I

thought I had filled my shirt out quite nicely today. I never looked beyond my shoulders, though.

But like I said, today I was on a roll.

Trainers, legs, butt, body. Then I accidentally got to my face.

I was stood in front of the mirror, looking at my face, but instead of feeling that need to push my eyes up, instead of feeling any pain or anger, that day in the gym I looked at my face and I smiled. Not just a small smile, though: a smile that made my cheeks hurt. And as I looked at my smile, I noticed that I have one dimple on the right side of my face.

For the first time in 20 years, I saw my eyes, I saw how blue they were, and I thought, *I love my eyes.*

That right there was an energy shift that changed my entire life.

It wasn't planned. It came at the most unexpected of moments.

Nice trainers, sparrow legs (let's be honest), cute butt, body (sometimes full of ale, sometimes full of kale), and now I could see that I have an epic face!

With this new-found energy, being able to show up more as my authentic self, I started to live with more confidence.

I didn't put pressure on myself either.

*

But somehow, I still got it wrong sometimes.

I ended up dating someone who had a boyfriend and she kept saying 'Why isn't he as nice as you?', 'Why doesn't he treat me like you do?', 'I wish we were together.' But she never left him. I even remember her calling me up one night, needing a lift home. It was 2am, so I grabbed my car keys and headed into town. I rang her and told her where I was, hoping she'd finished with her boyfriend and actually wanted to see me. Instead, she climbed into the back of my car with another lad she had met and I took them to his house. I acted like this was OK. I dropped them off and sped off in anger – I got my first speeding ticket that night.

I dated another girl. Again, we were never exclusive – there was a bit of a pattern here. I wasn't introduced to parents, I was never 'official' with anyone, I was always on the periphery and even with my new confidence I was struggling with thoughts like *Who's ever going to want to be with me and show me off? My birth parents couldn't do it, so how can anyone else?*

I was experiencing good things, but I still kept on getting these random kicks in the gut that brought me back to reality, that brought me back to that crazy routine, and every now and again I'd get nervous about seeing my face in case I had lost that new energy and love for it, (although thankfully I never did from this point on).

Then I met a girl in the gym where I worked. We had a laugh together and I often found myself ignoring all my tasks and talking to her for ages instead. I liked her, and I knew she liked me as every time I did a health check-up on her and checked her heart rate, it would start beating like crazy. It was the sweetest thing. We started dating.

She met my family and friends, and I met hers. Our friendship groups soon mixed and we went on this amazing ride together.

We began to grow together, and I was able to be myself. We were both in our early twenties and were able to explore and experiment in life together as we had a safe place.

My friends and family loved her too.

We did everything together and she became my partner for nine years. I don't want to downplay the massive, beautiful impact that she had on my life, but as we are no longer together, I won't be going into the details. We grew apart. There was no nastiness, no falling out, we had just grown to want different things.

This person is an amazing human being and she allowed me to grow in the safest environment. We had adventures, love and so many happy memories. She is one of the biggest superheroes in my life. I was able to share life with her and I can never repay her for the growth that she enabled me to do while we were together. Not all exes wear capes!

She even saw my crazy routine and accepted it. She challenged it too and reminded me that I didn't have to do any of it: I felt loved and fancied however I showed up.

We bought our first house together, bought cars, had holidays and lived a life of carefree luxury. Anything we wanted, we were lucky enough to do – though saying that, we worked our butts off for those things. We worked hard and created a life together.

But like I said, it ended eventually. There was no anger, no hate. We just grew apart. Looking back, I was still growing. I still had so much work to do in finding who I was. I hadn't found my purpose. I wasn't happy and sought out new challenges and adventures.

The relationship led to new personal growth, though: a growth that empowered me to start sharing my thoughts and journey with the world.

My partner and I were in Egypt when I was reading one of her magazines. There was an article making fun of a celebrity's appearance: they called it the 'circle of shame' and they highlighted areas of the body that the celebrity should be ashamed of – wrinkles were circled, cellulite highlighted. I read it and it angered me. I thought, *This right here is what's so wrong and toxic about our media*, and it heavily influenced and emotionally tortured me.

Towards the end of this article it said, 'Have you got a story to tell?'

And I thought, *Hell, yes, I have.* So I wrote to the magazine, sharing my growth, sharing my face, the one with the dimple when I smile!

I once thought I was unlovable and unattractive, yet here I was in Egypt with a total babe. I was going to show the world my face and how amazing life can be when you turn up as your authentic self.

My story – our story – was published and went viral. The BBC picked it up and loved our energy. I'm saying 'our' and 'we' because my partner was a massive part of this.

The BBC sat us down and wanted to do a documentary about us – they wanted to share our energy with the world, and we accepted. We filmed for nine months, creating a piece called *Love Me, Love My Face.* It was a documentary where they followed us as we went through the process of trying to find my birth parents (which I'll go into later).

We were on the same page too – I wanted it to be raw, open and transparent: however it went, I wanted it to be real.

And it was. We created something we were all incredibly proud of.

I was empowered, building more self-love, and I was able to pass that on to others.

The more self-love I had, the more opportunity pre-sented itself. The more self-love I had, the more power I had to manage my emotions.

Once the documentary was complete, we started doing promos for it – photo shoots and interviews – and it was amazing. So many people loved us, yet we were just this normal couple.

Before the show came out, we went on *BBC Breakfast* to promote it.

It was a short interview and was broadcast repeatedly throughout the day before being posted on the BBC's website.

We watched it back online and then opened up the comments section. There were so many amazing com-ments, but this also became my first experience of internet trolls.

'Why is she with him?' was the comment that hurt the most. The other jokes were things I'd heard before – these were once my own thoughts – but as I saw her reaction to them, I hurt even more. That protector came out in me again. The following week our documentary was going to be aired nationwide on prime time TV and this now scared me.

ITV got in touch and invited us onto their mid-morning breakfast show and we agreed to do that. It was crazy and mad, but we went with it and the interview was beautiful, funny and engaging. Once we had finished, our phones were blowing up, full of love and respect. Again a video was posted online and I had to see the comments. But this time I felt ownership, I felt the love and respect. People loved the fact someone was turning up as their authentic self and had found love within themselves and from another.

As for the trolls, I was finding new ways of processing this – more on that soon.

Our documentary aired and was a huge success, eventually reaching audiences all over the globe, and the world responded with love.

The best bit, though, was that families with facial differences started reaching out, asking me to visit them and speak at their schools. So, without any hesitation I did.

When I was invited to do my very first talk in a school, I was nervous, I was scared, but I was now able to do those things that scared me.

I arrived at the school feeling kind of OK. But then as soon as all these tiny humans started to walk in, the nerves grew and grew.

Tiny humans can and will say absolutely anything.

Hundreds of them soon filled an entire assembly hall and were sitting cross-legged, staring at me.

What the hell was I doing back at school?!

The teacher introduced me and all the kids together in harmony said, 'Good morning, everyone. Good morning, Jono.'

The nerves grew, like they did at the bar a few years earlier.

I looked at the floor. My bottom lip shook as I spoke.

No more hiding. I was going to get through this.

I shared my journey. I spoke of naturally celebrating who I was as a child, I spoke of my heroes, I spoke of the bullies. I showed them (and dropped) my hearing aid and I shared that now I love my face.

They all cheered and clapped, but tiny humans clap and cheer at anything, so deep down I thought I had failed.

The school bell sounded, and all the kids went out into the school yard and I headed out for my taxi.

As I stood outside waiting, a couple of kids ran up to me and asked to see my hearing aid. So I showed them, and they were like, 'That's so cool, I wish I didn't have to listen to my newborn baby sister cry.'

More kids ran over. 'Sir, can you play football with us, please?'

I said yes and then they started arguing about whose team I was on.

More kids ran over, and I couldn't really play as I was surrounded by so many of them. They started sharing stories about when they had been bullied. They were telling me that they didn't know their mums or dads, and finally one girl rolled her sleeve up to uncover her hand and showed me that she had been born missing a finger. She told me that from *now* she wasn't going to hide it any more.

All the kids cheered again.

I had no idea what was going on, but I knew that I needed to do more of this.

A teacher came to tell me that my taxi was here. I said my goodbyes and thank yous, and I left with my heart feeling full and hopeful that sharing and connecting can help others in finding self-love too.

As I walked to the car, the teacher looked at me with a smile and a few tears in her eyes, proceeded to thank me and gave me the biggest hug.

In one moment your life can change for ever, simply by being open to connect with those around you. To this day I don't know what she thanked me for, I don't know what those tears were from, but I felt it so much.

The more I shared my story and my thoughts, the more people responded with 'I've felt like that too.'

Being able to normalise this kind of stuff was life-changing.

It was insane. It was magical.

Life became so full of the most random and unexpected adventures all over the world.

I was totally unprepared for it and so were the people around me. But we rolled with it – well, I tried to!

I began to visit schools and families all over the world. By helping and supporting others, I was so full of self-love and I wanted to share that with everyone I could. It was what I had needed when I was younger, and if I had got that then, maybe I would have been able to find self-love at a much earlier age.

But by doing this I think it masked problems and traumas that I hadn't fully overcome yet, and as we rolled with it all, certain traumas kept on coming back to bite me. Or maybe it was the fact that I wasn't finding time for myself to do the work. Remember, you can't pour from an empty cup.

Is there anything in your life that you haven't revisited in a while? For whatever reason, is there something that you've been putting off?

Some of these questions may sound similar to before but as you read, you may have lightbulb moments or you may have triggers that are going off – they're all around us, try not to ignore them. We need to start facing them like the superhero that you are becoming!

CHAPTER 8
LOOK AT HOW FAR
YOU'VE COME . . .

Before I delve into this chapter, I want to emphasise that comfort, routine and a safe place are important. I don't want to lose that message.

A routine and safety net created the best environment for me to reach out to my birth parents, and that safety net saved my life when I hit an unexpected low in my thirties (more on that later).

Up until this point I've not spoken about my two birth parents.

Throughout my entire life I have thought about these two people. I knew nothing about them, so had even made up backstories for them; they were in a band, my dad played guitar and my mum would sing. They had blond hair and blue eyes, and sang songs about love.

As I got older, as I became filled with anger, I hated my birth parents more than anyone and soon their blond hair had faded and their eyes had gone grey; they sang about darkness.

During my teenage years I wanted to hurt them as much as I was hurting, if not more.

On every special occasion, such as birthdays and Christmas, they would enter my mind and I would hurt. Every little thing that I achieved would hurt more because I couldn't show them.

Then I developed a weird, unhealthy motivation tactic. If I was ever struggling to do something, I would say to myself, *Prove them wrong, show them how ace you are.*

It worked, as it generated adrenaline and an anger that spurred me on, but long-term this way of thinking made my feelings worse.

Much later, when I was in my nine-year romantic relationship and things were good, thanks to my safety net and a healthy routine, I felt like I was in the right frame of mind to explore my beginning in life and hopefully reach out to my birth parents.

I'd always had so many questions. *Who are they? Do I have siblings? What do they do? Where do my blue eyes come from?* That whole nature vs nurture debate – I was intrigued by it all. But ultimately by my mid-twenties I just wanted to reach out to them to let them know I was OK. That was the main goal. I'd spent so much of my life hating them that I wanted to make sure they knew I didn't hate them now and that I was living a good, happy life.

I wanted to do it properly, with the right support. My mum and my partner knew all about it and were 100 per cent behind me. My friends knew and were there for me in whatever way I needed them to be.

I contacted a local adoption agency and met with a lady who worked there. At our first meeting she listened to me, she answered all my questions and if she didn't know the answer she said she would try to find out. The first session was about getting to know one another and seeing if I was in the right space to explore reconnecting with my birth parents. It was always a team effort, and after that first meeting, I felt prepared to proceed.

The next step was the agency gaining access to all my paperwork. The agency worker went through it on her own first, so she could prepare me for what was to come. She sat me down and she was incredibly honest. She told me my birth parents had been through a lot and were clear that we needed to go our separate ways, which had caused a rift in the family. (Remember my secret grandma.)

She asked me if I wanted to read the paperwork.

I did.

I read that they had gone on to have further children – *I have even more siblings*, I thought.

I found out about the village I would have grown up in. (It wasn't as cool as Featherstone, though.)

I saw my birth certificate with my original name on it. I read what jobs my birth parents had and what their passions were.

For the first time in my life, these two people weren't stories that I had made up. They were real.

The lady gave me some time to think about what my next steps would be.

I sat with it. I already knew what I wanted to do, but I spoke to those around me. I was getting better at that.

I remember talking to my mum about it and she was so incredibly supportive but joked, 'You won't leave me, will you, when you find them?'

I gave her the biggest hug and reminded her that she was my mum and nothing would ever change that.

I decided I was ready to proceed. I wanted to make contact with them.

This was a massive decision in my life, and I could only have gone ahead with it once I had let go of the anger, had the right people around me and could be open with them about my thoughts and feelings.

We all put a letter together, stating that I was OK and

that I was open to meeting them. It was sent in the post and we waited. The agency said they would ring me if they heard anything.

For a moment the 'whys' came back.

Why did it have to come to this? Why has this happened?

I couldn't think of anything else during the wait. Nothing else mattered.

As much as I tried to carry on with life, my phone became my obsession.

One evening, my phone rang and I saw that it was the agency. I answered.

The lady on the phone asked me how I was doing. I said I was fine. There was no small talk as she knew that I was on edge while waiting to find out what the response was, and she went straight into saying, 'Jonathan, I'm afraid they do not wish to have any contact with you.'

She invited me in to see her, we made a date and I thanked her and hung up the phone.

I cried. I went to tell my mum and gave her the biggest hug. My partner came down and saw me and instantly knew what had happened.

How could a parent leave a child behind in the first place, never mind reject them a second time, later in life?

I knew those feelings as I'd been there before.

But today I was hurt but I wasn't angry.

My birth parents did what they felt they needed to do for themselves and for their family.

I guess my thoughts would have been different if I didn't have those two people beside me right then. My reaction would have been different if I hadn't had all those epic heroes in my life.

In that moment, I really appreciated what I had and felt incredibly blessed.

I had tried. I was loved. My life went on.

For a while after that, everything seemed to be going fine. I had my family, my partner, my friends. I had a good routine. I was in my mid-twenties and felt settled and secure. I was still growing but was lucky enough to do some amazing things and make some life-changing connections. I was finding new things to love about myself and continued sharing my life with my heroes, plus I was meeting even more along the way.

I was progressing in every aspect of life, which was great, but while I was on this wave I didn't check in with myself at all. I didn't give it any thought. It didn't even enter my mind. Amazing things were happening and I didn't really allow myself to properly celebrate them. I was too eager to move on to the next challenge. I think celebrating my wins and being proud of what I have achieved is something I still need to work on.

After the success of the first documentary, the BBC approached me to do more and it was in areas that I was passionate about so I was like, *Yes, let's do it!*

In these programmes we covered topics that meant so much to me: starting a family and what my options were when it came to that, and helping people find and connect with their birth families. These were huge things in my own life, things that I had struggled to process and overcome. And if I felt like that, I'm sure many others did too. We approached these documentaries with that same raw, transparent energy we had with the first one and again they were well received by people all over the world.

Unfortunately, I was exposed to more trolls. One day, I opened up my social media to see that someone had sent me a link to a website and said, 'Hey, dude, it's you . . .'

I clicked the link, and it took me through to a joke website. The site set a topic per day and then everyone made up jokes about that topic.

Today's topic was me and I was now looking at a photo of myself on this website. Below my photo was the comments section. I moved my cursor down to it and clicked to read on.

I was now glued to my computer screen reading hundreds of jokes making fun of every aspect of my life.

It hurt. It sucked. I felt myself wanting to protect my mum, my partner and all my friends from these awful comments.

As I continued to read, I found comments that were the same as the thoughts I had once believed about myself. Since thinking these things, I had healed. I now looked at myself with love and respect and as I thought about these people, all hiding behind a fake image online, I couldn't help but feel sorry for them. I used to think my face would prevent me from finding love and happiness: the truth is that it's attitudes like theirs that prevent you from finding love and happiness. I felt sad for them because they don't see all the beauty in the world like I do. They hide behind fear and hatred. They're scared of showing the world their authentic selves and that's just sad.

I wonder what they would would have to say if they saw an image of themselves on the screen? I wouldn't want them to write down a joke or nasty comment, but I certainly would want to challenge them to write something down that they love about themselves.

Do you think they would be able to do it?

I logged off, wanting and believing I could grow even more. Nothing was going to stop me.

At this point, I was on a roll, and I was incredibly blessed that the documentaries afforded me many more opportunities. I got nominated to carry the Olympic torch during the 2012 Games in London. Someone had nominated me for the work that I had done over the past few years and it was another surreal moment in my life. To this day I still can't believe it happened.

I got to walk in catwalk shows, speak to audiences all over the world, and make and present more TV programmes. I became an ambassador for various charities that are close to my heart, and I continued the work in schools – one of my favourite things to do.

Soon I had all this 'success', and it created a wave of temporary happiness. I needed more of it. Year after year, I needed to do more, be bigger and better, otherwise I felt I was going backwards. I needed to raise *more* money for charity, I needed to do *more* school visits, I needed to meet *more* families. I wanted to help and I wanted to give because I knew how much it was needed. However, my own cup was getting emptier yet I continued to pour from it regardless.

It became a drug. It had replaced my need for a person, my need to entertain. Now I felt I needed to inspire, to give love, in order to be seen as someone who was confident and successful.

It felt like I was on a hamster wheel, running as fast as I could, and I couldn't get off because if I did, then I wouldn't be able to get back on. So on and on I sprinted, going round and round.

Life continued that way for a while. For years, I felt like I had to say yes to everything. I showed up, I smiled, I loved and I gave it everything that I had.

I still hadn't discovered boundary-setting and couldn't recognise where my lines were when it came to people outside my circle. Progress was still to be made in this area.

Looking back, I see now some people were able to take advantage of me. My ideas were stolen, my time and emotions were used for others' agendas, but I agreed to it.

Despite all the challenges I was facing personally, we were changing the world and I was able to be a part of so many incredible projects.

I was investing so much time and energy outside of my relationship. At home I felt safe, but I wasn't investing time and energy into my personal life. With all that was going on around me, I neglected this area – not intentionally, but because it was OK I just didn't bother. My partner continued to support me through it all.

I eventually became frustrated and I wasn't happy. I felt fake. I felt like I was living in a glass house and wanted to break free from it all.

But I was scared to voice how I felt because I didn't want to break the safety net and routine that we had created. I was scared to say no to things because I didn't want it to end or change. It was a battle that I didn't know how to approach.

My relationship was something that I felt I ignored and wasn't able to truly invest in for the couple of years towards the end, and this is something that I've found very hard to admit and write down, because I failed one of my heroes. Not on purpose, but I felt we were growing apart and I didn't act or talk about it. Our friends were moving forward in their relationships though. And I remember thinking at the time that asking someone when they are having kids or getting married can be a hurtful or disrespectful thing to do.

When my walls have been up and I've needed some kind of inspiration, music has always spoken to me and helped me get the hardest of feelings out. Later on in the relationship, late one night, I was driving home from an event I had spoken at. It was a four-hour drive back home. I was tired, emotional – I always am after a speaking event. I'd spoken about my life, I'd shared stories about my joys and traumas, and on the drive home I felt it all again. I had the radio on, and I heard the beautiful haunting tune of 'Wasting My Young Years' by London Grammar.

The lyrics spoke to me so honestly and it hurt. *I'm wasting my young years.*

I cried, I felt pain and I felt guilt.

I was in this internal war trying to fight this weird battle of not living for my needs but doing things that I felt I needed to do. Somewhere I had lost my values – too busy people-pleasing, world-pleasing, showing up every day for others but not myself and not always those that mattered.

I thought the world of my partner – and still do – but was I holding her back? *How do I navigate this? How do I do the work? How do I show up? How do I make this right? What is right?* I was lost.

I pulled over at a service station and just cried.

I was scared to make a change because I didn't want to be alone. I didn't want to lose a friend, my safety net, my life. I felt selfish and horrible.

After four hours and hundreds of miles, I finally arrived home. I pulled up to the drive. It was gone midnight and all the lights were off.

I turned the engine off, and I didn't know where to go. I just sat, I don't know how long for.

I eventually went in and quietly got ready for bed, hoping not to wake her.

The next morning, we woke, we spoke, and it was back to the normal routine . . .

But I started having panic attacks because I couldn't stop stressing and thinking about my situation.

I started doing yoga and meditation to try and process my thoughts, to try and cope with my anxiety. It helped, it really did, but I still had to sit down and make the change.

I got into a routine of doing yoga every Sunday, and one day after yoga I was in our spare room getting changed. In that moment I realised what needed to be done. It was the start of my partner and I going our separate ways.

I knew it was right, but for weeks afterwards, I was so scared. I questioned what I had done. I wouldn't say there were regrets or that I wanted her back, but that safety net had gone and that scared me. That routine had gone and that unsettled me.

Deep down, though, I knew it was the right thing and it was long overdue.

Since this break-up, I've grown and dealt with things that I never had the opportunity to do.

More than ever, I've realised that routine and a safety net kept me safe but prevented further growth and healing.

I needed to be alone, and I was for two years.

I travelled to the furthest of places. I met strangers in the most random places and made connections with people I wouldn't have met if I hadn't left that safety net behind.

The more I discovered myself, the more opportunities presented themselves.

I grew in confidence and was able to say no. I was able to understand my boundaries, I was still winging it in life, but I didn't feel the need to please and say yes. I was gaining control. I learned that my energy is precious and only I can control where it goes.

I continued to raise money for causes that meant something to me. I went about it discreetly and always had the mindset that whatever amount was raised was huge.

I continued to visit families, still sharing life moments with them. All these families from all over the world sharing their lives and moments with me makes me feel incredibly fortunate. I feel like now I have family all over the world and the world has really become my home.

One night I was having a few beers with that same hero who got me a bar job all those years ago, and he casually said, 'Start up your own charity, mate.'

So I did.

With my lifelong friends, I set up a charity. As I was travelling and meeting all these families, I was able to support them emotionally, but as I visited countries with fewer resources I met families who couldn't afford medical support and were relying on funding or health insurance, but sometimes the insurance that was designed to support them turned them down. I wanted to do more.

I had already been working on smaller, similar projects with another friend and together we set up the Love Me Love My Face foundation. Today, we help families living with facial differences all over the world by offering emotional and medical support.

When it came to designing a logo, I had a vision of using my silhouette because anybody who has Treacher Collins would recognise that. I approached another life-long friend, who is a tattoo artist, and she somehow saw what was in my head and created an amazing logo that people instantly recognise as us. Together, we've gone from strength to strength.

I've gone from questioning and thinking that I needed to do something in order for people to be my friends, to actually believing in something and discovering that those same friends want to actively be involved in it. I love that growth in me.

I've been able to see the world and do the most random, amazing things. I've bungee-jumped off harbour bridges, I've visited hospitals, I've tried some bizarre foods, I've been asked for a selfie and an autograph by border security as we drove through the Andes into Chile. I've hiked up the tallest of mountains. I've done so much in this world with people that I once thought hated and judged me, but I see love and connection everywhere I go, through celebrating who I am.

But the weirdest thing was that when I got home after the amazing stuff, or when I was living my day-to-day life, my feelings would catch me off-guard and kick me in the gut again.

I'd be home from an event and I'd be cleaning the house or doing the weekly shop and I would just cry. Emotions would take over every part of me and literally pour out of me through tears.

Something was still amiss. I was still not able to fill my cup when I needed to. Or I was doing it when it was too late. Despite everything appearing to be going well on the surface, I would soon find out how quickly everything can come crashing down, and the safety nets that I had established for myself would be pushed to their limits.

In my mid-thirties I had a year where I felt that everything I touched turned to gold. I regularly had to pinch myself as life felt so good in every area: I celebrated self-love; I trusted my boundaries; when I played football, I scored a few goals and played well; when I trained I felt fit; when I visited the cake section at the supermarket I'd choose the biggest cake and eat it all; when I was doing charity work, people listened, they offered support and they donated; my relationships felt healthy; I enjoyed time on my own and time with other people; my career was progressing; I had savings in my bank; and even did some DIY projects on the house. All areas of my life felt healthy.

But one January it all came crumbling down within weeks. A relationship ended unexpectedly. Then a few days later I received a phone call to say that my mum had collapsed. As I rushed to her house I remember seeing her from afar lying on a stretcher and being wheeled into the back of an ambulance. My heart sank. I rushed to the ambulance and even though she was in pain and embarrassed, and not really sure what was going on, she was still smiling and reassuring me. After a bit of time in the hospital she fully recovered, but it was scary for us all. I have always feared what life will be like without my mum and for the few days that followed I was lost in my thoughts. It felt as if people were leaving me again and I had no control over it.

A few days later, as I was driving to the gym, I hit a car side-on. Thankfully the other driver and I were both OK, but emotionally I was a mess.

I was hurting and felt pain and sadness in every waking moment. I just wanted it all to stop and go away. I didn't want to feel any of it any more, I just couldn't manage it. I would drink alcohol daily, but looking back that only made things worse. There was an evening where I drank a bottle of whisky and passed out. I remember waking up with a pain in my chest and a tingling in my left arm. I sat up hoping that I had just laid on it funny, but it got worse. I got up and walked around the house. It didn't get better. I took some paracetamol and sat down, waiting for it to kick in, but as I sat there I started thinking again, *Why me? Why is all this happening to me now?* I was scared and it all became too much.

I rang 999 and they sent out a first responder. He sat me down on my sofa and asked me to focus on my breathing. He answered my questions and within a few minutes I felt calm and the pains went away.

He left and I went back to bed, but as I lay there I cried.

The following day all the emotions were still there, but I fell back into not speaking to anyone about them. I went completely within myself. I remembered that fake smile that I once wore and put that back on. I got through the day by surrounding myself with people, but once I was alone again, I had these moments of just massive sadness that would make my heart race.

The evening came and it was the same pattern: more alcohol and falling asleep, and then waking up with the exact same pain in my chest. This time I remembered what the 999 responder had said, so I went back and sat on the same spot on the sofa and focused on my breathing. Thankfully my heart rate settled and the pain went away.

I headed back to bed exhausted and feeling defeated. *How do I stop all this?* I wondered.

The following day my heart still didn't feel right and I was fighting to try to keep it settled, but no matter what I tried to do, nothing was working. So I took myself to A&E. I dealt with this entire situation on my own. I don't know why now, but I just didn't even think to ask for support. It's something that I'd been preaching for years but it didn't even enter my own head.

At the hospital, I gave them my name and told them why I was there. The lady behind the counter gave me a reassuring smile and asked me to take a seat in the waiting room. I felt OK at this moment, like I was going to get some kind of answer and everything would be fine.

When I was called to see the doctor I told him what I had been feeling in my heart and chest. Again, I kept the emotional side out. It's scary how quickly all the unhealthy coping strategies can come back.

He said that he would run some tests to see what was going on.

I sat there and after a while they ran a few tests and kept me in a bay. I paced around that bay until my results came back. *Something has to be wrong with me and they will find it,* I thought to myself.

After a while a doctor came over to me. 'I've been watching you for the past half an hour,' he said. 'You've not been still for a single second. What's going on?'

I said I was anxious about my results. He said they came back a while ago and that everything was fine. 'But I've been watching you and I'm concerned.'

I said I was fine, that it was a relief my results were clear and that that would help me. But he wasn't convinced and he advised me to take care of myself emotionally. 'Go talk to someone,' he said.

I thanked him and headed out.

I ignored his advice and on my way home I bought some more the alcohol and watched a movie to try to forget it all. The movie mixed with alcohol triggered all kinds of emotions: my heart raced, I sweated, I raced around the house, I cried. The feeling of wanting it all to stop consumed me again. I took myself to bed, curled up and just cried, hoping for it all to end. Eventually I fell asleep and had a temporary break from all of the shit that was taking over me.

But then, in the early hours of the morning, I woke up and every feeling of pain and sadness hit me within seconds.

Putting a stop to these feelings was all I could think about. I remember being in the kitchen and looking at my knives. *People end it like this,* I thought, but I was too scared to touch them. I then remembered someone from the news who had tragically taken their own life, I became obsessed with details, *How did they find the right time and location to end things?* And finally, *How do I get to that point? How do I end this?*

Fortunately reality kicked in and those thoughts settled. I sat and felt numb. I picked up my phone and called a suicide helpline. The man on the other end listened. I don't remember receiving any advice or doing anything in particular; we simply had a conversation, and after that conversation I went to bed and eventually managed to fall asleep.

The following morning I knew I had to do more. I knew I had to share and open up. It started with my friends. I typed a long message explaining the past week, including everything I had felt. I shared everything with them, not leaving a single thing out. It was an essay and I proofread it several times, all the while thinking, *Shall I just delete it or shall I send it?*

I decided to press send and chucked my phone down.

I was scared to read what would happen next, to find out what they would think of me.

My phone started pinging with messages.

And as I read them they were all full of love and support. My friends and I arranged to meet up more regularly, outside of the boozy get-togethers, and have meals together and just connect again. And we did.

Soon after, my doctor rang me. It turned out the A&E doctor had informed my local practice what was going on and shared that he was concerned about my wellbeing. My doctor asked me what I was going to do about it, and together we worked on a plan. We decided I needed more help, so along with yoga, exercise, meditation and being open about my feelings with those around me, I decided to see a therapist. It took me a few attempts to find the right one, but once I did they were able to support me in doing a lot of the work that I was missing, neglecting or wasn't aware needed to be done. We still have sessions that can leave me unsettled, but overall going through this therapy has been huge and I would definitely encourage everyone to try and work it into their lives if they have the means.

(Therapy isn't for everyone, though, and there are other ways of getting support. You can find some of these in the resources section at the back of the book.)

In time, I told my family about what I'd gone through. After that, I uploaded a shorter version to my socials – we're in this together!

From this whole experience I've taken away a couple of things:

Firstly, I've realised that when I have heavy emotions going on, alcohol doesn't help me at all, so I stay away from it.

Second, I realised that life, our mental health, physical health, can literally change in a moment. Now, I'm not suggesting wrapping yourself in cotton wool, but I always try and remember that however happy I may feel, however safe I feel, I should still continue to check in with my emotions, so I'm best prepared for whatever life throws at me.

Who or what makes you feel safe?

What does your ideal routine look like? One that makes you feel strong, able to withstand the tough times life might throw at you?

Are you making the time to check in with your emotions?

Are there any relationships in your life that you are holding on to because you're afraid of losing a part of your safety net? Do you feel free enough to grow and be your authentic self?

CHAPTER 9
LESS IS MORE?

By the time I had reached my thirties, I felt I was doing those huge life-changing things but more importantly I had more control of how and when I needed to fill my own cup. What I learned and needed to process was that life is full of the smaller stuff and these things need to be acknowledged and felt just as much, if not more. It was these things that were able to keep my cup constantly full.

It's not possible to do the massive stuff every day. It's not realistic and, most importantly, it isn't grounding.

Shortly after I received the news about my birth parents, a family that had a little girl with Treacher Collins reached out to me, asking if they could meet me. I jumped at the chance. This was exactly what I had needed when I was a child: to meet someone with the same condition, to see someone who had confidence, a smile, an energy that showed me some light at the end of the tunnel.

As I travelled down south on the train to meet them at their family home, I reflected on my birth family and their rejection. I thought about my secret grandma. I felt loved, and I was excited and nervous to meet this family.

I wanted to be a shining light, I wanted to bring hope, I wanted them to see a future of happiness.

But I wanted to be real with them too and not sugar-coat anything. I had it all going on in my head.

When I arrived, I was met at the door by the mother and her daughter. I couldn't help but smile. I was invited in and we spent the morning bearing our souls to one another. Unfiltered thoughts and feelings were exchanged. The family had two children, and we drew pictures and hung out together.

I still have the drawing that little girl did for me that day. That single drawing grounds me like nothing else. There was no agenda, no motive, just a kid's drawing that we did together.

When I left, I knew I needed more of this stuff in my life. More families reached out and every time they asked what I wanted to do, I thought of that visit and said, 'I want to do everything that you do as a family!'

It goes far beyond that now and I really appreciate my days as they come:

That morning coffee and how amazing it feels.

Barefoot walks in my garden or in a nearby stream.

The memories that a song can bring.

A random message popping up on your phone.

The taste of your favourite food.

Watching nature and all its beauty.

The moment you realise you have something in common with someone.

Talking to someone and realising they just 'get it'.

These things surround me on a daily basis and sometimes I miss their impact if I'm somehow obsessing over the next big goal, so I really work on appreciating these things more than ever.

I've discovered some powerful connections with myself and the world around me when I've embraced the 'small' stuff, which actually turns out to be quite massive.

I was invited to do a talk about self-love in the United States and, during that weekend, I met someone.

I arrived late at night, checked in and headed straight to bed. Looking at the schedule, I clocked an early morning yoga session the following day and I thought that would set me up perfectly for the next few days.

The next morning, I woke up and put on my leggings and vest before heading to the lobby.

I saw a lady standing in the reception area. She was also wearing leggings and, not really thinking about anything else other than my yoga class, I assumed she was the teacher.

I walked up to her and asked her if she was the yoga teacher.

She went bright red and said, 'I'm not, but the class and the teacher are down there in front of the hotel.'

I thanked her and walked off, not realising I'd accidentally given her the best compliment.

Over the next few days, I was in work mode. I always am when I travel: focused on the cause, focused on the families, focused on spreading self-love.

This lady and I would often find ourselves sat next to each other, or gravitating towards one another.

Neither of us acted on it and we returned home, me to the UK and her to her home state.

But a small feeling lingered and I reached out.

We got talking and that small feeling grew.

And I know what you're thinking: repeated patterns, seeking out a relationship again.

But you see, I'd grown. I'd done some healing. I wasn't lonely this time, I wasn't seeking affection or love, I didn't feel like I was missing something. I wanted to explore this little connection and I believe you should have the confidence to do that.

We were talking and obviously very aware that there was a giant pond between us, but I was showing up as my authentic self and I believe she was too.

I was 34 and a new empowering confidence was running through my being.

So, after a late-night phone conversation with her, I sat there, and I thought to myself, *I am going to ask her out.*

So, I did. I asked her out on a date.

She said yes.

Well.

OMG, YES!

That night, I booked a flight to the States and the following week I flew over that giant pond to take her out on our first date. Well, she picked me up from the airport first and the date proceeded from there.

She drove us to town for some food.

She pulled up outside a restaurant and I couldn't wait any longer. I kissed her right there and then in the parking lot.

We went for margaritas and tacos and spent the best week together.

I have a tattoo on my Achilles with the number 4,628 down the back of it.

Those numbers stand for the miles I flew to share a date with this person, but they represent so much more than just a distance; they mean connection – not just romantic, but any kind of human connection that can be made at any given moment. They helped me to realise that I'm attracted to and seek connections that fill my life with epic energy, and those connections go so much deeper when I'm my authentic self, full of self-love.

It's like a superpower that can make anything happen.

We had a crazy, amazing two years together before it ended. There was growth here: we didn't plod along or rely on routine. We opened up, we shared it all and we took action, even if that final action was to go our separate ways as a romantic couple.

We still talk and are both left with our epic memories and connection.

The reason I shared this story is because I really had to focus on the day-to-day smaller things in life to get me through this period. Whenever I visited, it felt like a big countdown and that we should do something ace together because I wouldn't see her for another month, so the small things really took on a big value in my life.

I'd gone from hiding away in my bedroom to seeing the world.

When people ask me what my favourite country is, I will always think about the incredible people I have met along the way and that always influences my answer.

Life is about connection and when you're full of self-love, you attract the best connections. You're equipped to tackle anything that life throws at you!

CHAPTER 10
WHAT *REALLY* IS
SELF-LOVE?

What is self-love?

There's a difference between arrogance, faking it till you make it, and real, deep self-appreciation. I believe that self-love is being able to love ourselves physically, emotionally and spiritually. Self-love starts with being kind to ourselves, filling our bodies with fluids and good foods while also allowing space for treats. Self-love is enjoying our bodies, allowing them to move and be free, without the constraints we put on them with our own judging eyes. Self-love has boundaries that keep us safe. It's having dreams and goals as well as having the confidence to pursue them.

I want you to have so much self-love inside you that it bursts out of you, protecting you from the bullshit that the world can at times throw at you, so you can be your own hero!

Why is it important?

There are times when you're all alone.

Your heroes have come and gone.

Your health may not be what it once was.

You may lose your income.

That safety net may be taken away from you.

Whatever happens in your life, every night you go to bed with a head full of thoughts and a heart that's beating *only* for you.

I'm not saying you should be alone. I encourage you to surround yourself with love. Be open to the heroes that you can meet on any given day. But most importantly, work on being your own hero, full of superhero self-love, and that will best equip you to take on and connect with everything our beautiful world has to offer.

What will self-love bring you?

Let's look at why it is so powerful and what it will bring when you welcome it in:

Lasting, long-term happiness.

More meaningful relationships.

Freedom from social pressures and expectations.

A career that brings you satisfaction over success.

More energy, a new lease of life.

This has continued to open doors for me, presenting me with opportunities over and over again.

It's enabled me to meet the best friends. And supported me in finding the best love.

I once pushed away all my heroes and a darkness took over my soul, leading me to hate everything I once celebrated as an innocent child.

I believed that my face would hold me back from all the things I wanted to achieve in life.

I believed I didn't belong in this world.

So I hid away, full of hate and the darkest of thoughts.

I didn't have a single ounce of love inside of me.

And I believed every person in the world didn't get me.

But today, I'm so full of love that people feel it when I'm around them. I feel it flowing through my body, from when I wake up to when I finally close my eyes at the end of the day.

I love all that I am. There's no more hiding. I'm out on

my next adventure while appreciating all the small things between.

But how did I reach this point?

Well, it didn't come from cosmetic surgery. I was asked about this for a large chunk of my childhood years and for various reasons I declined it, and I'm so glad I did. I know it works for some people and that's OK, but my choices have led me down a very different road.

That growth didn't come from a filter that you find on a social media app or camera setting.

It didn't come from fake tan or a crazy diet.

It didn't come from fancy clothes or a fancy car – well, a boy-racer Clio.

It didn't come from a bottle of whisky or sex.

It didn't come from another that I once desperately sought.

It didn't come from me dropping my boundaries and people-pleasing.

It didn't come from relying on a safe, easy routine.

Yes, at times I experimented with all the above and found temporary love and happiness. But it was often fragile, fake or very short-lived and then I needed the next fix of something from the list above to feel happy.

But in the long run, relying on those things alone held me back as it prevented me from doing work that needed to be done.

The true lasting growth and love for myself came from within, it came from me. At times from the deepest, hardest-to-find places that are inside all of us.

My heroes definitely helped me to keep going, often giving me hope when I thought it was lost.

This in turn passed on to me and with that hope I was able to take control and do some work for myself.

I spent time with myself and felt every emotion possible.

I got to know the reasons why I was feeling like that, even when it scared me.

I shared my feelings with others, and through this I was able to file and process certain emotions that enabled me to let go of the hate.

I put myself out there and met and spoke to strangers, who gave me faith in humanity. I put myself in situations that I feared, and I survived and then conquered them.

I have learned that diversity should be embraced and celebrated because our uniqueness is what makes us who we are.

The super-amazing souls in this world are attracted to the *real* you.

Hate will attract hate and love will attract love.

Through all that, doors opened, friendships grew and my love for myself got bigger and stronger.

I'm still on this journey and there are days when my light fades, but there are sparks inside me that continue to ignite my self-love and this beautiful world we live in.

It comes from within and it's inside every single one of us.

I want you start writing down a daily or weekly gratitude list of all the things that you are grateful for. They can be big or they can be small.

For example, I'm grateful for having a safe place to sleep tonight.

I'm grateful that I have been able to invest my time in ways to look after myself.

I'm grateful that I am able to drive and have the independence to travel around on my own while listening to my favourite tunes.

There are so many things around us that we can take for granted but when you start actually listing them, you realise how many things there are to be grateful for. This exercise helps you feel more positive, and those good vibes help us become our very own hero!

CHAPTER 11
HEALING THOUGHTS

By sharing all the scary stuff that I once hid deep within myself, and through discovering and exploring things that I love about myself, I can now look back at areas that once caused me so much pain with a much different, more powerful, healing mindset.

Every time I was stared at, called names or laughed at, I often wondered what I could do to fix it or stop it, and I looked inwards, at myself: *What could I do or change?* But the truth is, it was never down to me.

I wasn't bullied because I have a facial difference.

I wasn't bullied because I wore a hearing aid.

I wasn't bullied because I wore my glasses wonky.

I was bullied because the other individual had hate or sadness inside them that was slowly destroying them.

If only I had realised this when I was younger!

As social media grows, so do the trolls, and I think we all can experience some kind of hate, whether that is directly or indirectly targeted at you.

I feel sorry for those who carry around all that hatred. They don't see the world the way I do. They don't see the beauty I do, they don't experience the connections that I get to experience, and I feel truly blessed to be able to live through my adventures and make connections with so many epic souls along the way. There's so much more to come and this excites me so much.

And now, to my final thoughts about my birth parents.

I've often asked myself why we couldn't have stayed together.

In my head they have always been in that band – their appearance may have changed, but I always felt that they loved one another.

I've had days where I thought that they left me through love, for them, for me.

I've had days where I thought that they left me through hate. *How could they do this to me?*

Thankfully, the hate has long gone.

On my birthday, at Christmas or any other special milestones that I proudly reach and celebrate, I often reflect on life. I think of my birth parents and I send positive thoughts and love their way.

You gave me life; you brought me into this beautiful world and gave me the opportunity to live and celebrate it.

You were my beginning; you created a new life that's mine to fill with love and adventure.

And I do, I do, I do – and as I do, more epic adventures lie ahead. I'll discover more self-love, I'll share the stuff that makes me sad and I'll meet more epic strangers in the most random, unexpected moments and any one of them could be a hero, who doesn't wear a cape, just like you!

My healing thoughts also recognise that there is always work to be done, that we are never fully healed. As I write this, I feel like I've done so much work on myself. From day one I faced rejection, from day one I grew up with a difference that everyone could see when they met me. This has forced me to do the work from such a young age. Although, as I've said, there were times when I chose not to do the work, I ignored it, I did everything else except the work.

So, yes, I'm in a really good place right now. I know who I am, I love who I am, I celebrate who I am. I am open about my feelings. But there is still work to be done. I guess there is always work to be done and we shouldn't be afraid of that.

Recently I faced a break-up (the one I briefly mentioned earlier). The effect it had on me uncovered even more work that I needed to do.

In any new relationship, as well as in the relationships I currently have, I turn up as my authentic self. I'm very clear with my boundaries. I share my love languages, my dreams and my hopes. The other person needs to match my energy, and I genuinely felt that had happened with this person. Things were going well but then she opened up and told me she could no longer do it and our relationship ended.

Break-ups suck and this sucked.

However, what I noticed this time was that when she called it off, I found myself loving this person even more; the fact our relationship had ended didn't stop my love for her from growing.

I asked why. I wanted to know why I did this.

I spoke to my therapist and he advised me to do some work on my inner child.

When I spent a year discovering the things I love about myself, I also spent some time working on my inner child. To help myself with this, I got one of my old teddies and put one of my old rugby shirts on him. I spent time with him, listened to him, talked to him. He went everywhere with me. He became Little J – and I loved him and his ridiculous haircuts so much.

So, when my therapist made this suggestion, this time I knew straight away what I needed to do.

I was doing a photo shoot and it was a two-hour drive

away, so it was the perfect opportunity to spend some time with Little J.

I packed my snacks, sat Little J on the passenger seat, put on some tunes and off we went.

I went straight into it: *Why do people keep on leaving us? Why do we keep on getting rejected?* These were the things that I was obsessing over during this particular break-up: *I'm a great guy, I feel I'm a great partner, so why do people keep on leaving?*

I'm very aware during break-ups that we don't always get the answers or explanations from the other person and, sometimes, we're not entitled to them either. My main focus was on me and what I could do to work through this.

As I was driving, I began to go through the times we were rejected. That came naturally and I cried. It hurt, it sucked. The list was long, the pain was deep.

But then after a while I thought: *Hold on, what about the things and especially the people that you attract?*

I've had break-ups and new relationships have started, amazing relationships that ended on good terms. Relationships that I'm incredibly blessed to have experienced. All of a sudden, I was thinking of and feeling all the other epic things that I've attracted: family, friendships, opportunity, life.

Little J, all who you are, all this self-love – we attract so many epic things, real authentic connections, and going forward we will continue to attract so much more, all while you keep on being you!

I'm 37 now, and I turn up as my authentic self. I'm still doing the work and there are still times when I will slip back into some of the unhealthy coping strategies I've previously spoken about, but I'm full of self-love.

In fact, as I've mentioned, in 2021 I found 170 things that I loved about myself. I bet no one in the world has found that many things that they love about themselves and I challenge you to beat it. But be warned: since then I've made it a daily practice, and I'm still adding to my list!

But like every type of self-care that we do, at times we can't go there, it's too tiring. So that's why we need to show up and be open to the moments and people that can change our lives in the best possible way.

We can go forward with the love found within ourselves, be our own hero and use those extra superpowers available to us. And we can also generate love and adventures from the environment as well as those people around us.

> So with all that in mind, what do you love about yourself?
> As a child I started with a few items on my self-love list.
> As a teenager I just had a self-hate list.

Now, my self-love list is so long, I've lost count of the total. It ranges from things that I see today to what I see when I visualise my inner child.

Remember, sometimes our self-loves start with likes and when we can't find them that's OK too. Sometimes they won't come, and sometimes a friend or even a random stranger can help us find them.

Explore stuff that you can see and explore the stuff found deep within you.

Daily journaling is really helpful in just getting clarity on the things that are causing you pain.

Please, let me get you started on how to get in touch with your inner child as this has been a massive benefit to me.

To get started, grab an old photo of yourself. If you find one from when you were in a dark place, had negative thoughts, or felt unlovable, embarrassed or ashamed of yourself, that is useful. If not, close your eyes and visualise yourself during a dark period in your life.

I want you to look at this image. Who are you looking at?

For me it's the 14-year-old boy standing in front of the mirror hating his face.

Now, talk to your inner child and ask them this – how do they feel about the way you treat them now? And how does that make them feel?

Now ask your inner child this:

What do they need from you right now and going forward?

I want you to listen to your inner child and give them the biggest hug because together you are going to become the biggest hero your life has ever seen!

Further Resources

Love Me, Love My Face Foundation

Instagram: @love.myface

Facebook: www.facebook.com/LoveMeLoveMyFace
   Foundation

Happy Place

Website: www.happyplaceofficial.co.uk

Instagram: @happyplaceofficial

Mental health crisis helplines

Samaritans

Website: www.samaritans.org

Phone: 116 123 (free from any phone, open 24/7 and
   365 days a year)

Email: jo@samaritans.org

National Suicide Prevention Helpline

Phone: 0800 689 5652 (6pm–3:30am every day)

SHOUT

You can text 'SHOUT' to 85258 for free from all major UK mobile networks. You'll then be connected to a volunteer for an anonymous conversation by text message.

NHS: Urgent mental health helplines (England)

Find a local NHS urgent mental health helpline in England by answering two questions at the link below.

Website: www.nhs.uk/service-search/mental-health/find-an-urgent-mental-health-helpline

Charities supporting children, victims and people with facial differences

Barnardo's

Founded in 1866, Barnardo's is a British charity that works to improve the welfare of vulnerable children, specifically those up for fostering and adoption.

Website: www.barnardos.org.uk

Victim Support

Victim Support is an independent charity dedicated to supporting victims of crime and traumatic incidents in England and Wales.

Website: www.victimsupport.org.uk

Phone: 08 08 16 89 111

Face Equality International

FEI is a global alliance of charities working to promote the
campaign of face equality and to support and represent
people with facial differences.

Website: www.faceequalityinternational.org

Meditation and mindfulness resources

Calm

www.calm.com

Headspace

www.headspace.com

Therapy resources

Andy's Man Club

A men's suicide prevention charity offering free-to-attend
peer-to-peer support groups across the United King-
dom and online.

Website: www.andysmanclub.co.uk

Turning Point

A charity supporting people with their drug and alcohol
use, mental health, offending behaviour, unemploy-
ment issues and people with a learning disability.

Website: www.turning-point.co.uk

Mind

Website: www.mind.org.uk

Instagram: @mindcharity

Infoline: 0300 123 3393

Substance abuse resources

The following resources are organised by region. Follow the links below to find meetings and support in your area.

Drink Aware

Website: www.drinkaware.co.uk

Alcoholics Anonymous UK

Website: www.alcoholics-anonymous.org.uk

Al-Anon UK

Website: www.al-anonuk.org.uk

Acknowledgements

First of all, I want to thank the two people who gave me a life to live.

I want to thank my family for laying down the best foundations that enabled me to fill that life with adventure.

I want to thank all the other children that shared a home with me, becoming my brothers and sisters.

My friends, for always being there, loving all the versions I turned up as.

I want to thank my hairdresser for finally giving me a decent haircut.

I want to thank the strangers that I've met along the way that greeted me with a smile.

A big shout-out to all the mums who've made sure I've eaten at events. And to the dads that have always made sure I've got a drink in my hand – you know who you are.

The whole team at Happy Place and Ebury for supporting this project. We did this together.

And finally, a huge thank you goes to me.

For being brave, for doing the scary shit, for not giving up when that felt like the easiest option, for seeking out adventure, choosing the biggest piece of cake, for loving all that you are – a badass with an epic heart.

Oh, and thank you to YOU, the person reading this book, for now being part of my journey too.